A Big Manhattan Year

Tales of

Competitive Birding

DAVID BARRETT

CONTENTS

1

INTRODUCTION

To do a "big year" in birding means to try to observe as many bird species as possible in a given geographic area in a calendar year.

The term nearly made its way into the popular lexicon in the fall of 2011 with the heavily marketed Steve Martin comedy *The Big Year*, which was loosely based on Mark Obmascik's fine nonfiction book of the same name, whose subject was the record-setting North American big year competition of 1998. The movie did much less well than expected, perhaps because it was more a drama than a laugh-out-loud comedy, and birding quickly fell back out of the spotlight.

North America north of the Mexican border (plus ocean waters up to 200 miles offshore) is the broadest commonly-contested area over which birders in the United States attempt to have a big year. Some prefer to the limit themselves to the continental 48 states.

There is no need to cover such a wide area, of course. You can choose to do your big year anywhere you want: your state, your county, your city, your favorite local park, or even your own back yard. If you want competition, though, you need to consider where other people are birding and how their records are reported.

The first question people ask when I tell them how a big year contest works is, "How do you know the birders are not lying about what they see—do they have to take photographs?" It is all done on the honor system and no photographs are required, though some birders do take them. In fact, it is not even necessary to *see* a bird—*hearing* its distinctive call or song also allows you to count it.

Central Park is a world-famous birding location, and it is where I spent nearly all of my first year as a birder. Jeffrey Kimball's excellent 2012 documentary, *Birders: The Central Park Effect*, beautifully showcases both the park's birds and its many birders. It is, however, far from the only good place to go birding in Manhattan, a borough that abounds with parks and other public locations for birders to explore.

This book follows my progress as a birder chronologically, from my first birding walk in November 2010 to my first "little" big year in 2011, and then to the main focus: my 2012 Manhattan big year in which I competed against other top birders using the popular online checklist site eBird[1].

Before I could compete at birding, though, I first had to become a birder. Here is how that happened.

---

[1] eBird is much more than just a way to keep checklists online; it is a free, easy-to-use, worldwide database of bird observations with many real-time charting and mapping functions. By using it, you will contribute to science and gain access to information that can make your birding more productive and enjoyable. Without it, this book would not have been possible. I highly recommend it and discuss it more in Chapter 12.

2

A WAY TO IMPROVE MY RUNNING?

In the summer of 2010 I visited Central Park for an hour or two nearly every day, as I had been doing for over a year. I was not looking for birds; I was running.

A few months later, I would take up birding in order to become better at running. Does that sound farfetched? The logic goes like this: to become better at running, I believed that I needed to walk more; to make walking in the park less dull—so I would do enough of it—I decided to look at birds while doing it.

That summer marked my tenth year as a competitive middle-distance runner. My best race was the mile, and I was preparing again, as I had in many summers past, for one of the world's best-known road-mile races, the Fifth Avenue Mile, usually held in late September just a few blocks from where I lived on New York City's Upper East Side. I was grinding out a set of ten 75-second quarter-miles on a measured segment of Central Park's East Drive.

I was a serious amateur, able to run a low five-minute mile, a good time for a masters (over-40) athlete. I was constantly looking for ways to get better.

I had my own library of books on training and physiology. I followed a training plan, from *Daniel's Racing Formula*, that had worked well for me before. I logged every workout, down to my heart-rate and time for each 1,000-meter interval, as I had since the beginning. I wanted every advantage I could get.

The mile requires two attributes: speed and aerobic ability.

I had plenty of the former. Genetics and resistance work had given me strong quads. I could sprint well as a schoolboy, and it took very little training for me to sprint well again as a master.

Aerobic ability, the more important attribute, was something I had to build—I certainly was not born with it. I still recall the agony of completing the so-called "twelve-minute test" in gym class when I was fifteen. Why, I thought then, would anyone want to run without stopping for twelve whole minutes?

Truly talented distance runners have mainly slow-twitch muscle and exceptional cardiac output. I appeared to have plenty of fast-twitch, and scans have shown that my heart's stroke volume was average at best, even after years of training.

For health reasons I had taken up easy running in my early twenties. Running two to four times per week for about 20 to 30 minutes was enough, along with occasional light gym workouts, to keep me feeling and looking fit.

By my late thirties I felt that this easy routine was no longer working. I began to tire more easily, and I did not subjectively feel as fit as I used to.

To push myself to a higher level of fitness—and to test my abilities—I decided in the spring of 2001 to try competing at the mile, a distance I selected because it would most reward my inherent speed, yet it would also demand serious endurance training. I increased my weekly mileage, and extended my longest run to 75 minutes. I trained specifically for the one-mile race, and my debut went much better than I had expected, despite only a few months of training. I was hooked, and running became the new focus of my free time.

Within another year I had worked up to doing two-hour Sunday runs. Though I still performed best at the shorter distances, my training had built the aerobic endurance that I had previously lacked. I occasionally dabbled at longer-distance races, even as far as ten miles.

Training 35 to 50 miles per week (including two race-pace interval sessions) had numerous benefits. I became leaner without losing strength; I looked years younger; and I felt more energetic.

Running was a healthful adjunct to a life that required a great deal of sitting. I worked as a trader and hedge fund manager. Not only did I sit in front of computer screens during trading hours but I also sat while riding the Metro-North train to and from Connecticut for an additional two hours every weekday.

Right after trading finished, usually around 4:30 or 5:00 in the afternoon, I would put on my running clothes and head outside to train. It was a great way to break out of trading mode and keep my mind and body sharp.

In early 2009 I made a major life change: I left the firm I had helped establish to trade my own capital, right out of my apartment. The long commute was over.

Improvement requires recovery from hard efforts, and recovery requires sleep. My more flexible schedule immediately allowed me to get more sleep, and it showed in my running performance. I set lifetime personal bests in 2009 at the four-mile and five-mile distances.

But my mile time of 5:23 in 2009 was actually a second worse than I had run the year before, a performance that had been hindered by one of the most bizarre and stressful weeks in market history, that of the Lehman bankruptcy. With better rest and better performance at the longer distances—and no financial apocalypse to cause anxiety—I had been expecting to run a much faster mile. What happened?

I had an idea. The logs that I kept showed my training was

nearly the same with a bit more emphasis on speed in the latter year. There was a hidden training element, however, that my logs did not track: walking!

In 2008 getting to work meant walking to the subway, riding it to 125th Street, walking to the Metro-North station, riding the train and then walking another half-mile to the office. Altogether I did at least a half-hour of daily walking. With a new bedroom-to-living-room commute of 25 feet, I was missing out on a lot of walking and — crucial to a distance runner — the mitochondrial development that comes with it.

Why not just run more, you might ask? Running is even better at building mitochondria, and 45 miles per week is below average for the most serious amateurs. But I often tried running more, and my legs did not recover from it well enough to handle speed work. A few weeks of higher mileage would leave me overtrained and worse off than when I started. Even slow running causes microscopic muscle tears. Walking briskly causes much less muscle damage and still provides a small training stimulus.

So in the summer of 2010 I resolved to replace all of the lost walking and more. I would end my training runs on the west side of Central Park, forcing myself to stroll home through the Ramble. Doing so gave me time to appreciate the natural beauty of Central Park, something that was easy to miss when I was running all-out.

I usually stopped running just west of Belvedere Castle. From there I would walk the path up to the castle and continue east, moving just south of Turtle Pond. I noticed that signs marked this route as a "nature walk," so I looked for examples of nature! I saw mostly squirrels and the occasional Mallard walking on the grass (the Mallard was the only duck I could reliably recognize).

Did the extra walking help me run faster? My training appeared to be going very well, and test workouts suggested a new personal best was within reach, but an August throat infection followed by an abdominal strain kept me from racing in September. Though I had my training logs as evidence of the fitness I had achieved, I was disappointed not to have earned a competitive result.

This was not the first time I saw great training wasted. In 2002 I might have been in sub 5:00-minute mile shape but illness struck days before the race and I ran 5:12. In 2007 I was again in top form but then "overtraining syndrome" came on and I had to pull out. I trained punishingly hard, always aiming to set a personal best, but this approach brought with it a high risk of physical breakdown.

My mile times were good enough to win many state-level masters competitions in those days, though not New York's. I wanted to keep racing as long as I could continue improving, but I sensed that after a decade of serious training I was nearing the limits of whatever minor talent I had.

Perhaps the additional walking would help me extend those limits just a bit more.[1]

I was preparing to finish the 2010 road-racing year with a 10K, a distance at which I had not previously competed, in December, and I was finding the training less fun than in the past. Running fast requires pushing through the pain, and I used to revel in it. Now I was still doing it but with less enthusiasm.

I was enjoying my walks in the park, though. They were quiet, relaxing, painless, and unpressured. They were also dull! I wanted to make them more interesting. I had learned years ago to identify trees, but it was late November and the leaves were gone, making identification tricky. I needed something else to

---

[1] Subsequent results showed the benefits of walking. During some months I would bird five or more hours most days and do only 15 miles of additional running per week. Yet my heart rate at easy running pace would fall to the lows I experienced during my 50-mile running weeks, indicating excellent aerobic fitness.

engage me.

It occurred to me that people also went to parks to look at birds. I decided to explore this option, but I did not hold out much hope for it. New York City had pigeons, sparrows, gulls, Mallards, robins, and a couple of very famous Red-tailed Hawks. Maybe there were ten species in total—how interesting could that be?

3

BIRDING BASICS

I figured someone must have made a list of the birds you can see in Central Park, so I began by searching the web for "Central Park bird list."

The first hit was a checklist developed by the Central Park Conservancy called "The Birds of Central Park." I was struck by the first sentence:

"This checklist includes the 200 species of wild birds regularly seen in the park since 1886."

200 species—really? I had lived in Manhattan for two decades and spent hundreds of hours in the park. I had not seen 20 species, much less 200. Where were these birds, and what did they look like?

The next hit provided an answer. Bruce Yolton's *Urban Hawks* site included his Central Park bird list along with his own photographs of the birds. Clearly the Conservancy was not kidding, as Yolton's list also had over 150 species. These birds were way more colorful than the pigeons and sparrows I was seeing. They were beautiful. I wanted to go out and see them.

Mr. Yolton is known for his excellent coverage of the park's Red-tailed Hawks, but he is also a top all-around birder. He was asked to give a public lecture in 2008 on introductory birding, entitled "50 Birds in 50 Days," and he keeps the slides from it available on his site. I started going through them. They began with the most commonly-seen birds and stated where in the park and at what times of year you might see them.

Right away I liked the idea of birding, how its demands were both intellectual (learning the field marks of a species) and physical (walking the park and actively looking). It occurred to me then that birding could easily become much more than a way to enliven my training walks. It would require assimilating a considerable amount of knowledge and building new skills. It sounded like something that could hold my interest.

His lecture slides provided enough information to get me started. The "Abundance by Season" list for early winter told me what species I would need to learn how to identify. References to Phil Jeffery's "Central Park Birding" site suggested that a good place to begin would be the area of Central Park known as the Ramble, approximately between 79th and 73rd Streets on the north and south, and between the West and East Drives. Since I lived nearby, starting with the Ramble seemed fine to me.

Phil Jeffrey's site is also the place to go to learn the special names given by birders to various key locations in the park, particularly within the Ramble. I use these names—such as Hernshead, Maintenance Meadow, Evodia Field, and the Oven—often, sometimes without explanation, in this book. As for the major bodies of water, any decent map of Central Park will name them; from north to south they are the Meer, the Pool, the Reservoir, Turtle Pond, the Lake, and the Pond.

The only part of Yolton's presentation that gave me pause was on binoculars, which appeared to be necessary for any birder. It stated that "excellent binoculars begin at $275 and go over $1,800." I did some research of my own on the web and found that this was true.

Still, I was not about to spend anywhere near even the lower of these two figures to try out a new hobby. I had some experience with optics. I had used telescopes costing less than $100 to get satisfying views of the rings of Saturn and the moons of Jupiter, objects that were many hundreds of millions of miles away. I figured that cheap binoculars would be just fine for looking at birds 30 yards away, and I was right.

I already had a pair of binoculars[1], purchased years ago for a visit to a golf tournament. They cost about $40 then. The incremental expense of using them for birding, since I already owned them, would therefore be $0.

This was another element of birding's appeal: it cost nothing to do it. I could learn all I wanted about it online for free, and Central Park did not charge admission. Thus I could take a day off from trading and not worry about replacing an income-producing activity with a money drain.

I took my first birding walk in the Ramble shortly before sunset on Sunday, November 28, 2010.

I had already picked up on the theme of list-keeping in birding, which was consistent with what I was doing to track my running progress, so I noted what I saw and put it on a spreadsheet afterward: Mallard, Northern Shoveler, Canada Goose, and House Sparrow. These are among the most common birds in the park, I had seen all but the Northern Shoveler before; their names, however, were new to me, and I was excited to observe them more closely.

My days had become too familiar and repetitive: get up, trade, run, read, and sleep. The birds of Central Park provided a source of unpredictable variety. Darkness came much too quickly, and I looked forward to returning the next day.

The following morning produced two exciting additions,

---

[1] They had a zoom feature and only a 25mm lens, so the field of view was tiny, and the light-gathering ability was poor. I had no idea what I was missing, though, and ended up happily seeing over 110 species with them before deciding to upgrade.

birds that I had never seen anywhere before: the Red-bellied Woodpecker and the Downy Woodpecker. True to their names, they pecked at the bark of trees, loudly enough in many cases to give away their locations. They were both handsome birds with vivid colors, the Red-bellied particularly so with its bright red cap and nape.

It occurred to me that I could have seen these woodpeckers long ago if I had just bothered to look. I had walked through woods many times, both as a child and as an adult. How had I missed ever seeing woodpeckers? They had been there all along, conspicuously so. Now I could see them all over the park, because I finally was *looking*.

I knew then that birding was going to be more than just a way for me to do additional walking. I had stumbled upon a gaping lacuna in my life experience, and wanted to fill it. I was going to have to make up for decades of not looking.

4

A RARE VISITOR DRAWS A CROWD

Tuesday, November 30, 2010, was a scheduled rest day from running, so I could afford to get to the park earlier and bird longer. I would skip an hour or two of trading.

My day began with a thrill: a Great Blue Heron wading at the edge of the island on Turtle Pond, by far the best bird I had seen so far and uncommon for late November in Central Park. At the time I saw it, I did not know for sure what it was, so I made mental notes of its features. Its long legs and neck left only a few possibilities on the page of bird photographs to which I referred after returning home, and I was soon sure of its identity.

I wandered further in the Ramble and, though I was not seeing many birds, I was having a great time. The terrain was hilly and challenging and I did not yet know where the paths went, so I could enjoy the thrill of entering new places

During warmer times the Ramble bustles with tourists, children on ranger-led nature walks, dog walkers, runners, and of course, birders. On this cool, overcast November day, the Ramble was mostly empty. I enjoyed some much-wanted solitude. It felt as if the park were my own expansive back yard.

I even managed to get so disoriented that in trying to exit the Ramble I circled within it, ending right back where I started.

There was no grid to follow; trees hid directional cues provided by the Manhattan skyline, and overcast skies hid those provided by the sun. If you like the feeling of not knowing you are in the middle of a densely-populated urban area (and I do), the Ramble is a good place to go. The North Woods of Central Park offers an even deeper-woods experience.

I set myself on a course northward and eastward and soon was passing through a lawn near 79th Street and East Drive known as the Maintenance Meadow. Suddenly I was no longer alone.

Gathered in the meadow were at least fifteen people, many of whom had cameras with huge telephoto lenses perched on tripods; the rest had handheld cameras or binoculars. They were waiting for something to appear, and I figured it had to be a bird.

I wanted to know *which* bird. I lingered for a short time, but the bird did not appear. So I went home and looked into the matter online.

Author and birder Marie Winn writes a blog about "Central Park Nature News." She already had the scoop. Two days ago, on the 28th, a Varied Thrush had been sighted in the Maintenance Meadow. It was a *vagrant*, a bird normally found in another region (in this case, the Pacific Northwest) that wandered off course. Just being a vagrant would make it interesting, but it was the rarest of vagrants, one with no confirmed prior records in Central Park. (There was one very likely unconfirmed record: Winn's site posted an email from a couple of birders who reported one in November 2003, but the bird could not be re-found by others the next day.)

The Varied Thrush quickly became the star attraction of the Central Park Ramble. It drew not just the regular birders of the park but also those from neighboring states like New Jersey and Connecticut.

What amazed me most about the bird was that, after traveling thousands of miles from its native habitat, it then chose to travel no more, remaining in a relatively tiny area. It could be seen most days on a patch of ground and weeds adjacent to the Maintenance Meadow's men's restroom, a plot roughly the size of a two-car garage. It occasionally was known to wander across the East Drive, but even then no more than a quarter-mile away.

It stayed for a surprisingly long time—from late November 2010 to mid-April 2011. To see it, you would show up in front of this patch and wait. There were benches nearby, and birders could employ team tactics, some watching while others sat. The wait could be three hours or more before getting a fleeting glimpse of the Varied Thrush at the back of the thicket. With an inaccessible area behind the men's room, the bird had no problem getting some privacy.

I would always take a quick look as I passed the area, but I had no interest in joining any waiting assemblage. Like the Varied Thrush, I also wanted some privacy.

In mid-January 2011 the timing was finally right: seed scattered on the ground to attract the Varied Thrush had brought together a collection of passerines including Eastern Towhee, a large, colorful sparrow with red sides. I peered in and within minutes saw a flash of orange—success! The Varied Thrush had become the most distinguished member of my small but growing "life list" (all the birds one has ever observed).

5

WINTER BIRDS

I was looking forward to ending my competitive running season with my first 10K race (thus achieving a *de facto* personal best) on December 5, 2010. It was windy and cold, and about three miles in I began getting side stitches that would eliminate any hope of a really good time. I gutted it out and finished with a kick. I was glad that the early start (8 a.m.) left plenty of time for birding.

Seeing my first Wood Duck, easily the most beautiful bird to grace inland waters, turned the day around.

I did not yet record every species I observed, just the new ones, along with the date and the location. Today I would consider this a minimal level of reporting, but then I was in only my second week of birding, and most days brought new species, so there was still much entering to do.

Winter in Central Park offers a decent variety of birds, many of which are around for most of the year and are considered relatively common. In summer there are too few species to make things interesting even for the beginner. The spring and fall migration seasons have the opposite problem: so many species pass through—well over 100—that beginner can be overwhelmed. Winter is an excellent time to learn to bird.

You want to start by learning the common birds well because

they are the ones you will see most often. You want to know them automatically and immediately, to be able to identify them from all angles and even in partial views. This takes experience.

The most common winter birds make things easy for the new birder by looking distinctly different from each other. Once you know them they are almost impossible to confuse.

This is not to say that learning them is totally easy. Consider the House Sparrow, one of the top few most frequently seen birds in the city. Males and females have different plumages, each of which can vary slightly in shade and intensity. I recall sometimes wondering if I was seeing a House Sparrow or some other (possibly more obscure) species that I had not yet learned.

To know the House Sparrow it also helps to know what other birds vaguely resemble it, such as the White-throated Sparrow. Then you find that White-throated Sparrows show even more variation: some have bright white throats and vivid yellow streaks above their eyes and others are more muted.

Another good thing about winter birding is that trees are bare and you can get unobstructed views of almost any bird you see. The challenge of identifying a warbler during the brief moments it pops out of leaf cover can wait until spring.

Central Park even offers you the chance to enjoy "bird theater," courtesy of the many well-maintained feeders at Evodia Field in the Ramble. You get close views with no walking required. As winter wears on, with cold and snow arriving, the feeders become more popular with a great variety of passerines.

You can expect to see:

Mourning Dove
Red-bellied Woodpecker
Downy Woodpecker
Yellow-bellied Sapsucker (occasionally)
Black-capped Chickadee
Tufted Titmouse

White-breasted Nuthatch
Brown Creeper
Fox Sparrow (occasionally)
White-throated Sparrow
Northern Cardinal
Common Grackle
House Finch
American Goldfinch
House Sparrow

If it is a finch irruption year, as it was in late 2012, you might also see Pine Siskin and Common Redpoll. These almost always would be considered noteworthy rarities.

Hawks often frequent the feeder area, too, but they do not care about the seed—they want birds! Look for Red-tailed Hawk and Cooper's Hawk.

To see waterfowl, go to the Reservoir (the Meer, Lake, Pond, and Pool offer more limited assortments). You are sure to see the three most common gulls: Ring-billed Gull, Herring Gull, and Great Black-backed Gull. You can also see a variety of ducks:

Wood Duck
Gadwall
Mallard
Northern Shoveler
Bufflehead
Ruddy Duck

along with Canada Goose, American Coot, and, if you are lucky, Pied-billed Grebe.

You can see that even in the middle of winter an experienced birder covering much of the park can tally 35 or more species in a single day. The Central Park Christmas Bird Count, where dozens of birders spread across the park to do an exhaustive count, had 59 total species on a single day in late December 2010.

My life Central Park list had grown to 46 by the end of February 2011. I still had a decent chance of expanding it every time I went to the park, and doing so provided a sense of accomplishment along with hard evidence that birding continued to offer new experiences.

I had always sought out activities in which I could measure my progress objectively. Mathematics, with the problem-solving contests I had enjoyed as a youth, was like that; so were my sports, such as golf and running; and so was securities trading. Being able to quantify my birding progress motivated me to continue learning more about the subject. I would study photographs and descriptions of species I had not yet seen to prepare myself to someday see them.

6

OWL QUEST

During the period November 2010 through February 2011, the *Urban Hawks* website occasionally featured photos and video footage of an Eastern Screech-Owl, which was said to live in the North Woods of Central Park.

Naturally I wanted to see this owl. The last time I had seen an owl, likely the same species, was in my childhood over thirty years ago.

Owls have a certain mystique about them. Most are nocturnal and solitary. Their calls sound eerie. They are hard to find.

This particular owl *had* been found and filmed—repeatedly, so much so that after awhile I felt that the *Urban Hawks* website was toying with me. It was happy to show me the owl doing all of its owl behaviors—waking up, rotating its head nearly 180°, coughing up a pellet of undigested bone and fur, calling for a mate, and flying out at dusk—but it would not say precisely *where* the owl was. You might think that the online message boards would have details, but they were also staying mum about it.

It turns out that many birders deem it unethical to publicly divulge the roosting location of an owl. The message boards even had explicit rules prohibiting such posts. *Urban Hawks*, a strong proponent of ethical birding[1], was simply trying to protect the owl from being harassed by inconsiderate observers. I will have more to say about this ethical issue in Chapter 35.

The issue of greater concern to me was a more pragmatic one: how do I find this owl?

I already had one clue: the owl was in the North Woods. The site said so.

This narrowed the search to an irregularly-shaped area at most 0.3 miles wide and 0.45 miles long.

The video provided many more clues: the owl roosted in a distinctively-shaped hollowed-out tree branch; the branch was split at its point of attachment to the tree; the viewing angle showed that the roost and the camera must have been roughly the same height, so it was a low roost; the tree had light-colored bark; the sound of running water could be heard. So the roost must be near the Loch (the small North Woods stream); and runners occasionally passed by in front of the camera.

Once I had the last clue, I figured it would be straightforward to find the owl. After all, I was a runner. I knew the running paths of northern Central Park well. The frequency of runners passing by, along with the sound of passing cars, strongly suggested that the owl was roosting very close to one of the park's blacktop drives. Of course, the dirt paths running across the park also drew a contingent of runners who, as I do, prefer to run on soft surfaces.

All I would have to do is run the park's drive, which looped the North Woods, and all of the trails near the Loch. I could come close to covering all of these paths in an hour of afternoon

---

[1] See the American Birding Association's website for their *Principles of Birding Ethics*. These are sensible rules that all birders should learn and follow. They do not specifically prohibit disclosing the location of an owl, however, but they do encourage the birder to first "evaluate the potential for disturbance to the bird...."

running. My binoculars, extremely lightweight and nearly pock-et-size, were easy to carry along.

Off I went!

On my first run I saw nothing resembling the hollowed-out tree branch. Maybe it was on a trail I had not run. Or perhaps I had run too fast and overlooked it. Next time I would be more careful.

I tried again. Being more careful did not help. Still, my train-ing routine called for an easy run on many days, so it was not costing me much to devote some of these runs to owl-roost re-connaissance. Maybe I would find other roosting locations—the owl had been known occasionally to move.

I must have run the North Woods at least a half-dozen times in search of the owl. I even ran at dusk once, hoping that the owl's call would lead me to it, or that maybe I would see Mr. Yolton doing his filming, but neither happened.

I decided that a more thorough walk, rather than a run, was needed. I also realized I had not given enough weight to the sec-ond-last clue. The sound of the Loch on the video was loud. Most of the Loch was quiet; only the a couple areas had falling water strong enough to make such a noise. I needed to focus on those areas.

I traipsed around the southern end of the Loch in dense brush. The water sound was right on, but still I saw no roost.

I walked out of the Loch and back up to park drive level. I turned to look back down and suddenly I saw it—the hollowed-out branch was right there! And so was the Eastern Screech-Owl.

The roost was within ten feet of the roadway, near the busy intersection of West Drive and the 102nd Street Transverse. Though it was high off the ground of the Loch, it was only a few feet above street level—just as the video suggested.

Thousands of runners and cyclists zoomed by every day. I myself had passed it at least a dozen times in just the last few months. The owl had been hiding in plain sight, in a roost so exposed, so obvious, that I never bothered to look directly at it.

I saw the Eastern Screech-Owl on March 2, 2011. *Urban Hawks* video showed it again two weeks later, on March 27, in a comfy new roosting hole. That is the last record of this owl in Central Park. It was never reported to be heard or seen again.

7

KINGLETS AND WARBLERS ARRIVE

By March 2011 I was feeling more confident about my birding skills. I had seen nearly all of the regular winter species and I could identify them readily, some of them just by their sounds. I knew, for example, the familiar *churr-churr-churr* of the Red-bellied Woodpecker. I had even posted some of my daily observation lists on the birding boards.

I also knew, however, that this was not the time for complacency. Birding was about to get *much* more complicated. Within two weeks the first spring migrants would start arriving in a trickle. Each successive week would bring more of them, species I had never seen before, many of which posed tough identification challenges. At the peak of spring migration, which for Central Park occurs around the first week of May, the Ramble might hold over 100 species, some 70 or more of which were not present in the winter.

I was not about to let the calendar take me by surprise. I had been poring over the list of expected spring migrants organized by how common each species was. I wanted to make sure I knew all the birds that one could reasonably expect to see.

To this end, I found the Cornell site *AllAboutBirds* extremely helpful. Each species had photos and a verbal description of field marks along with tips on how to distinguish it from other similar species. I created a "Spring Birds" document on my computer with photos and descriptions pasted in. I practiced putting a name to the photos, and also going the other way: seeing the name and visualizing the bird.

I remember clearly the morning of April 6, 2011. It was sunny and warm with very little wind—great conditions for seeing birds. I woke up around 8 a.m. to read a brief online post of good birding in the Ramble. By 8:45 I was at Belvedere Castle viewing the first Barn Swallows of the season. I recognized them from their dark blue backs, bright red throats, and forked tails. They were resting on the rocks below and then darting off over Turtle Pond to do their aerial acrobatics.

At Shakespeare Garden I nearly overlooked the bird for which I had come, having read about its arrival earlier in the online post. As I was ascending the path aside the garden I saw a small greenish bird flutter to my left. I was about to continue moving on when I realized this was a *very* small bird and therefore worthy of a closer look. It was a Golden-crowned Kinglet! It flapped its tiny wings with hummingbird-like quickness as it hovered near a pine tree, displaying its bright golden crown. I had never seen anything like it.

Nearly a week later a very similar morning began. After reading a report of a House Wren in Shakespeare Garden, I rushed out and caught a quick glimpse of it, noting its down-curved bill and faint eye-ring. I was not yet aware of what great singers the wrens were.

I had already seen a Carolina Wren quietly perching in low grass back in December. This is the easiest wren to observe in the park because of its loud, high-pitched, three-syllable song: *GERmany, GERmany, GERmany*, which can be heard at almost any time of year, even if the bird itself is not always easy to see. Only the males sing.

The House Wren has a much more complicated song, full of

trills and bubbling chatter, and both sexes sing during breeding season. The species is commonly seen and heard in Central Park from mid-April through May.

Belvedere Castle produced a Ruby-crowned Kinglet. Next to hummingbirds, for which they may at first glance be mistaken, the two kinglet species are the smallest birds that occur in the region.

The real thrill came from Tupelo Field, which held several small yellow birds with red streaks and red heads that pumped their tails as they moved on the grass: Palm Warblers—my first warbler species!

The pace of bird discovery seemed manageable, but now that I look back it is obvious why it was so easy: I was not spending much time birding, and I was overlooking a lot of birds when I did. Seeing birds in trees and brush takes practice.

I also had a problem with pace. I would go out for 90 minutes in the morning and then try to make it back for the stock market opening. I moved along too fast, likely scaring many birds on the way. Songbirds are sensitive to motion, particularly when it comes from large creatures such as humans. A fast stride is handy for traversing unproductive areas, but when you get to a place with birds you want to slow down and even stay still for awhile. Once the birds in an area do not perceive you as a threat, they may reappear and give you surprisingly close views.

As of April 12, my count for the year was 61 species. I should have been getting close to this many in a single day.

I was doing one thing right, however: I was making good use of the online postings and following up on them. When late afternoon reports came on April 14 of a Louisiana Waterthrush at the Upper Lobe and a Green Heron on Turtle Pond, I walked right out and got the birds.

The Louisiana Waterthrush is a warbler, but it appears where you might expect to find shorebirds, on the muddy shores of forest marshes and streams. It is less common in Central Park than its near lookalike, the Northern Waterthrush, with which it shares the habit of tail-pumping.

Central Park regularly gets three heron species. Black-crowned Night-Heron is most common, and a survey of the Lake's shore on a spring or fall day can reveal more than a few of them. Great Blue Heron can appear at almost any time of the year, usually alone; Green Heron appears only during the two migration seasons and is the rarest of the three.

I was getting into a habit that would serve me well in 2012 for my real big year: see the posted birds right away, before they are gone. Birders call this "chasing." I birded frequently and found many good birds through my own searching, but it made no sense to pass up the chance to see a rare bird whose location was already known.

8

PURSUIT OF THE LOON

On late Sunday, April 17, 2011, I read of a Common Loon re-ported on the Central Park Reservoir. It is a waterfowl that swims on the surface and then dives to capture prey. I knew this species to be rare for the park—seen only a few times per season. It sounded well worth getting.

The Reservoir is circled by one of the world's most famous running tracks, a 1.57-mile dirt path that affords runners pano-ramic views both of Central Park's largest body of water and of the surrounding skyline.

Looking for this loon would allow me to once again combine birding with my strength, running.

Unlike the North Woods, the Reservoir leaves birds with no-where to hide. It has no islands or structures on it, and the center of the Reservoir is never outside binocular viewing range. If the loon were still on the Reservoir I would eventually see it, and even a slow run with plenty of stops along the way for closer scanning would take only about 20 minutes. I figured this would be easy.

I would have to deal with one distraction, the Double-crested Cormorant. In profile, particularly at a distance, the cormorant looks like the Common Loon. Both float low on the water, have long bills that they angle slightly upward, and take frequent dives to catch fish or crustaceans. The Common Loon was said to be in breeding plumage, however, meaning it would have markedly different coloring: an all-black head with a white patterned collar and a white breast.

Nearly every morning someone would report that the loon was still being seen on the Reservoir. Yet when I ran the Reservoir, I saw no loon. Not the first time, which was only mildly disappointing; not the second time, which was more irksome; and not the third time, which left me tired and frustrated from seeing a long series of Double-crested Cormorants and no Common Loon.

I had a new "white whale," (my first was the Eastern Screech-Owl) and I was not about to let it get away.

I finally saw it on April 25 after over a week of trying. I did not even have to run. I searched the Reservoir on my lowest binocular magnification from the east side pump-house and saw a promising figure closer to the opposite side. I rested my binoculars on the guard rail for stability and upped the magnification to 27x. The white neck ring came into view, as did the black and white back. This definitely was the Common Loon.

Why had I kept missing it for so long? Maybe I was looking too close to shore. Common Loons have visited several times since then, and each time I have seen them at a distance, near the middle of the Reservoir—after only a few minutes of searching.

9

WARBLERS EVERYWHERE

After I found the Common Loon, the day continued to be productive. I added Northern Waterthrush and Belted Kingfisher, both at Turtle Pond, plus Gray Catbird and Wood Thrush in the Ramble. Getting five life birds in a day is one of the thrills of being a first-year birder.

The Belted Kingfisher is a regular but uncommon visitor to Central Park. It is a handsome, blue-gray, crested bird that emits a loud and distinctive rattle. It sometimes shows up to fish the small ponds of the park.

The Gray Catbird, whose name derives from its complicated calls, which some liken to a cat's mewing, begins arriving in Central Park in mid-April and by May it can be seen and heard all over the park. It remains abundant even during the summer, unlike most migrants, and then peaks again in September before departing. A straggler or two usually can be found in the park throughout the winter.

The Wood Thrush is striking both for its coloring—a bright, reddish-brown back and bold, dark-spotted breast—and for its beautifully eerie song, a fluted *ee-oh-lay* followed by an electric trill. The species is common only briefly, during May and then less so in late September and early October. Even at these times it is observed only in small numbers; three to five in a single walk is doing very well.

The following day, April 26, would also prove noteworthy. In retrospect, it was probably the peak of the season for warbler migration. Warm and sunny with little wind, the conditions were ideal for warblers to find insect food. There are at best a few days during migration when nearly every large tree in the Ramble has warblers on it, and where some trees have six or even more species. This was such a day.

As I was standing on the paved path south of Turtle Pond, I noticed a group of roughly thirty birders slowly moving toward me. Some of them were calling out birds:

"Pine Warbler on the right main branch of the large oak!"

"Northern Parula just below the Pine!"

I figured this group had to be from the American Museum of Natural History. I had read online about the spring migration bird walks that the museum offered, one of the most popular of which was led by Stephen Quinn, a naturalist and artist in charge of the museum's nature dioramas. I recognized Quinn, a trim, soft-spoken man with tousled brown hair, from a birding video he had done for the museum's website.

Up to now I had chosen to keep my birding entirely solitary. I enjoyed the time alone, and I also liked the "man versus nature" challenge of it. At the same time, though, I wanted to see as many birds as possible and develop more birding skills.

"Prairie Warbler, near the top of this tree!"

I moved quickly to get a look at what would be another new bird for me, found by Quinn and his group.

In less than ten minutes I had added three warblers, surely more than I would have found on my own. Moreover, I could list these birds with confidence, knowing that the species ID was confirmed by an expert with over thirty years of experience. I decided I would try to meet this group again next week.

My brief encounter with these birders had already taught me a lesson on warbler observation: I was looking too low and still moving along too quickly; I needed to wait patiently for movement in a tree rather than just glance at the tree, see nothing, and go on to the next tree. Many warblers feed very high, particularly in the early morning because that is where the insects are. It is true that Palm Warblers are frequently found on the ground, as are Yellow-rumped Warblers, both waterthrushes, and Ovenbirds. Black-and-white Warblers can be seen low on trees. The rarest warblers and most vireos, however, require looking high and courting the cervical spine pain known colloquially as "warbler neck."

I also needed to become more familiar with how warblers look from below. Photos online generally provide a full view of warbler plumage, which is aesthetically pleasing and provides the greatest detail. Sometimes you will get such a view in the field, but more often you will get a partial view—just the head and the throat, or just the throat and the belly, or even just a wing and a rump. The better you are at reasoning from such partial information, the more birds you can identify.

This is where having better optics can really help you. My binoculars had poor clarity and a narrow field of view. For large, reasonably close birds it did not matter. For faraway, tiny birds distinguished by intricate patterns, it mattered a lot. Too many birds were just a blur of yellow and white. Even those warblers seen well would move out of view as they danced across tree limbs, and I had to waste time re-finding them.

Stephen Quinn identified warblers quickly and confidently. His next walk added six birds for the year, including the rare Worm-eating Warbler, bringing me up to a respectable 84.

Often Quinn would call out a bird before he or anyone even saw it. He believed strongly in the value of birding "by ear," and he tried to teach this skill to members of his walks.

I could see how powerful this ability was. Everything conspires against people easily seeing warblers, but their songs (almost exclusively it is the male warblers that sing) uniquely identify them and can be heard regardless of leaf-cover or bird height. If you needed to find, say, a Prairie Warbler, it would be much easier simply to walk the Ramble and listen for its distinctive rising song rather than to try to sort visually through dozens of warblers in the trees.

It was late in the season for me to drill on warbler song, but I knew it was something I would want to do next year.

A good example of using sounds to locate birds came two days later on the May 5 walk. Quinn heard the squeaky song of a Rose-breasted Grosbeak, one of the most highly sought-after birds of spring migration. We were soon treated to good views of the large-billed male bird.

Quinn displays a deep reverence for and appreciation of nature, which he does his best to convey to members of his walks. At the same time, he enjoys putting his estimable birding skills to a competitive challenge and talked about how he was planning to attend the upcoming World Series of Birding at Cape May, New Jersey, a 24-hour "big day" event. He shows that one can be both a conservationist and a counter.

I was also getting good birds on my own in early May, such as American Redstart, Common Yellowthroat, Scarlet Tanager and—best of all—Lincoln's Sparrow.

The first two are among the most common warblers, abundant in both spring and fall.

The Scarlet Tanager is the far more common of the two tanagers that appear regularly in Central Park (the other is Summer Tanager, which I will discuss in Chapter 26). The male of the species in breeding plumage is a strikingly beautiful bird that everyone wants to see. It has a bright red body and black wings. It is easier to hear than to see, with a song described as scratchy or burry.

Lincoln's Sparrow is very rare in the park, and a bit easier to get in the fall than in the spring. If you bird every day you are likely to observe it at least once a year and maybe even a half-dozen times. It can appear where a grassy field borders a thicket, such as Wildflower Meadow or Tupelo Meadow.

Since my experience with following the American Museum of Natural History group had gone so well, I thought I would try another birding guide about whom I had read some very favorable things: Starr Saphir.

10

STARR SAPHIR

Starr's walks in the Central Park Ramble, given on Mondays and Wednesdays, met at 7:30 a.m. at the southeast corner of 81st and Central Park West. The cost was $8, paid in cash before the walk began. Starr also offered walks in the Central Park North End on Tuesdays and Saturdays. If you had not previously gone on her walks, Starr would ask your name. From this point on Starr referred to everyone by name and rarely forgot anyone. It was a feat of memory that I would see repeated often again in the following fall, sometimes with groups of over thirty birders. Someone once jokingly asked if Starr associated everyone's name with a bird. She did not.

Starr was 71 years old in May 2011, and she looked it. Before being stricken with breast cancer nine years ago, she had looked much younger than her age, according to those who knew her. She was very thin, appeared to be 5'5" tall, and had large, oval wire-frame glasses that she kept on even while looking through her binoculars—which were Zeiss. A blue scarf always covered her dark hair. She also always wore blue jeans and running shoes, and on colder days she would don a blue sweater or polar fleece. I later suspected that her theme of dressing in blue was a homage to her favorite bird, the Cerulean Warbler.

She walked slowly, bent-over forward (a back injury, she once explained), and she had a noticeable limp. Movement seemed to pain her. She would schedule at least two sitting breaks in every walk, one after roughly an hour, and another 90 minutes later. The first would be short, maybe five or ten minutes, and the second would be longer, usually fifteen minutes. She would take pain medication at these breaks and she would have a small snack on the second one. You might think she would never make it another two hundred yards, but she gave the longest walks of any birding guide in the park, almost always lasting four hours, and sometimes going six hours or more. She would end them when the group ran out of birds to see or when weather made birding impossible.

Her voice did not reflect any of these physical disabilities; it was clear and strong, somewhat low, and well-modulated, with perfect diction even when her thoughts came quickly, which they often did. It was the clear, commanding voice of a trained actor, which she had been in her younger days.

I did my first and only bird walk of the spring season with Starr Saphir on May 9, 2011. On it, Starr reminded everyone that she was undergoing chemotherapy treatment and that this accounted for occasional weakness.

Unlike the endings of her walks, the beginnings always took place within a minute of their scheduled times. Starr unfailingly showed up well beforehand, which entailed her rising at 4 a.m. or earlier on some days and taking a 45-minute subway ride from Inwood to the 81st Street stop by the American Museum of Natural History.

Starr made a point of exactly counting the number of bird species observed on each walk. For this purpose she had some help. Lenore Swenson, an excellent birding guide in her own right, who had learned to bird by joining Starr's walks in 1989 and who had attended nearly every walk for the past thirteen years, was the designated "scribe." She wrote down the species as they occurred and provided frequent updates of the total. She also aided in spotting birds. If Starr could not make it to a walk, Lenore would take over the lead. For these services Lenore received a share of the revenues.

Ever since Starr began birding in 1946, as a six-year-old, she had kept a written log of all her observations. The first bird she ever identified was a Black-and-white Warbler. Her records, written in a shorthand she devised, now filled dozens of notebooks.

Her methodology had remained consistent, something I learned after suggesting that since I had just seen a Cedar Waxwing while she was away, we could now add it to our count for the day. She did not doubt my sighting, but she said that a species could count on a walk only if observed by her or Lenore.

Starr loved to count birds, and on those days when Lenore was absent she would maintain the day's list of species entirely in her head, an impressive accomplishment given that the list was rarely shorter than 40 birds and sometimes 70 or even more. To get an exact count, Starr would sit down during a break and mentally page through the ABA Birding Checklist, which arranged species in groups of similar birds—such as Woodpeckers, Flycatchers, and Warblers—and call out the running total as she moved through it. Sometimes she would open up her printed copy of the list, but it was clear that she did not need to.

Starr amassed extraordinarily high lifetime species totals: 259 just in Central Park; 297 at Jamaica Bay Wildlife Refuge; 412 in New York State; 746 in the contiguous 48 states; and 2,582 over the entire world.

It was not only birds, though, that Starr identified and counted. She also knew all the butterflies and frequently stopped the group to draw attention to an unusually striking one, such as a Tiger Swallowtail or a Red Admiral.

Even more impressive, she knew the Odonates—the dragonflies. In June 2012 she visited Sterling Forest, and she phoned me with an account which I transcribed and posted online. She had noted 71 bird species and a great "many Odonates." A wildlife biologist wrote to me asking for a list of the Odonates that Starr had seen. I mentioned this to Starr, who suggested that I put the biologist in touch with her, as she had observed over 60 Odonate species and did not imagine that I wanted to relay that much information!

Bird species could start being counted on a walk as soon as Starr arrived. Despite the din of traffic on Central Park West, Starr frequently would hear several warblers while chatting with the group and waiting for the walk to begin.

Walks in the Ramble would proceed directly into the park from 81st Street and follow a dirt trail south and east to Triplets Bridge, a small wooden bridge over a narrow inlet to the Lake just north of 77th Street. From there, an excellent spot to see warblers, particularly waterthrushes, we would move further south to Hernshead, a small promontory on the Lake, where waterfowl could be viewed, along with more vireos and warblers in the trees.

Unless there was a special reason to visit Strawberry Fields right away, the walk would then proceed north, to Bank Rock Bridge, then across the dirt path at the Upper Lobe, another prime location for warblers and various other passerines (perching birds, including songbirds), and up to the benches by the Humming Tombstone, where the group would have its first short rest break. Starr would sit down and take payments from those who arrived late, but she would not stop birding; the tall trees to the south usually offered many species—flycatchers, vireos, and warblers—to keep the group busy.

We would then retrace our steps briefly, turn north, and ascend the path to Belvedere Castle. The lookout over Turtle Pond offered the chance for more waterfowl and possibly some swallows if the time was right.

Then we would follow the descending paved path toward the east end of Turtle Pond, usually seeing many passerines on the way in the trees surrounding the pond.

After this it was back south into the Ramble proper again, where the Maintenance Meadow restrooms offered everyone another chance for a stop. The meadow itself had sparrows and thrushes near the ground, and almost anything could appear in the trees and shrubs along the west border.

Then we walked over to Tupelo Meadow, whose expansive lawn offered the best chance in the Ramble for unusual sparrows, along with Ruby-throated Hummingbirds in the flower beds and passerines in the trees.

From there we walked further south by the source of Azalea Pond, where Starr always enjoyed finding huge bullfrogs. She told of how she had once seen a bullfrog entirely swallow a warbler.

Depending on what we were seeing, we might then visit nearby Evodia Field, just to the east, where feeders were maintained in the cooler months. Then it was back to Azalea Pond for the second, longer seated break, where the group could enjoy a snack while observing flycatchers and warblers flitting about the trees and over the water.

After the break, we would follow the small stream, known as the Gill, further west and then loop back east toward the Lake's small, muddy bay known as the Oven. This was a prime spot for waterthrushes, waterfowl and shorebirds. The trees could hold Rose-breasted Grosbeaks, Baltimore Orioles, and Scarlet Tanagers, too.

We would then follow the paved path west along the northern shore of the Lake across Bow Bridge, from which we usually walked east to Bethesda Fountain. This gave us the option of examining the pine trees of Cherry Hill or proceeding directly to Strawberry Fields, where we followed the dirt path north along the eastern edge and then finished the walk after returning on the grass to the south end.

All through the walks, Starr would display her staggeringly acute abilities to see and hear birds. Even with a large group, many of whom were experienced birders, she was generally the first to see a bird, and she would identify it almost instantly, even in poor lighting. She did not even need to raise her binoculars to identify most birds flying low overhead.

It was not that she had superior eyesight. On the contrary, she had cataracts and she peered through thick eyeglasses. It was her brain that set her apart. She knew where birds were most likely to be, and she knew exactly how they would appear, from any angle, and could quickly pick them out from a tangle of leaves and tree limbs. In the lingo of artificial intelligence, she had a powerful visual search algorithm and excellent pattern recognition.

Starr surely did, however, have superior hearing. She would often detect faraway bird song well before others heard it. In addition, she could perceive a number of competing bird songs or calls at one time and then tell you all of the species she was hearing. She not only knew warblers by song, as do many experienced birders, but also by just their chips—simple one-syllable calls.

She made her walks an educational experience by doing more than just helping people observe a lot of species. She explained bird behavior—how, for example, warblers would initially be found very high in trees at first sunlight because that is where the bugs were, and that as the day wore on one was likely to get lower views; or how Wood Ducks were so-called because they actually nested in trees.

She worked incredibly hard to make sure all members of her walks got to observe the birds that she found. Inevitably, though, some or even all members would occasionally miss a bird. She had a stock response: "I owe you [for example] a Cape May Warbler." Then she would do her best to deliver another

Cape May. She noted that her bird debts, as she called them, always expired at midnight in the event she could not repay them!

She believed strongly that pointing at songbirds was most likely to startle them and drive them away, a belief borne out often by results observed on the walks; she also believed that pointing did little to help other people locate birds. Instead, Starr encouraged her members to provide detailed verbal descriptions of a bird's location, and she expertly did the same herself. To make these descriptions easier to produce and follow, she suggested using the "clock" system on a tree, e.g., letting twelve o'clock be the apex of the tree and three o'clock be about halfway up the right side. She also suggested working one's way up from the trunk of the tree, noting if there were multiple trunks, and then indicating which of the main branches to follow to get to the bird.

Starr had a logical, analytical mind. She did the New York Times crossword puzzle every day, a pursuit that we shared. She approached birding as a scientist would. If she heard a trill that could be a number of different species, she would tell you the possibilities and how they might be distinguished, and similarly when she got only a partial view of a bird. She continued to read ornithological research and referred to it sometimes in answering questions.

Starr would become a most valuable mentor and ally in my big year quests of 2011 and 2012.

11

OPTICS UPGRADE

Birding had turned out to be more than a passing fancy. With fall migration already underway, and with me planning to spend upwards of 25 hours per week in the park, I decided in early September that it was time to get a decent pair of binoculars.

The ones I had were not fit for serious birding. They were cheap, compact binoculars for casual viewing. They let in too little light, and their field of vision was too small.

Binoculars are described by terms like 8 x 40, meaning magnification is 8 power (8 times) and the lens through which light enters is 40 mm in diameter.

I wanted the highest magnification generally found in birding binoculars, 10 power, as most of my target birds were relatively small with intricate plumage or, like hawks and shorebirds, just very far away. I also wanted a large objective lens, to allow as much light as possible and make colors vivid; a large field of view, at least 300 feet at 1000 yards; and the ability to focus at close distance, seven feet or less. Oh, and I was not going to pay more than $200!

I ended up spending a lot less than that, just $126, for the Zhumell 10 x 42 Signature Waterproof. I am totally satisfied with them. The image clarity and brightness are excellent. They have even impressed birders accustomed to using binoculars costing $500 or more. I wish I had had them for the spring migration season. I would have seen warblers more easily and better appreciated their beautiful colors.

12

DISCOVERING EBIRD

By September 12, 2011, I had observed 110 species for the year in Central Park. This seemed to be a respectable figure, but I did not know for sure. Birders sometimes reported their daily species totals on the message boards, but not their monthly or yearly totals. I wondered how other birders were doing.

I remembered the site eBird, on which I had created an account earlier in the year. It provides the user with front-end tools to enter one's birding observations into an online database. It also allows the user to search the database and get information about what other birders are seeing. It could produce real-time maps of species occurrence and graphs that showed seasonal abundance patterns. It strongly appealed to my quantitative bent. The feature of greatest interest to me, however, was its "Top Birders" list, which ranks users by annual species totals for given regions.

I wanted to see who the top birders were for Central Park (where I did all my birding), but this was not an option. The top birder lists were compiled only at the state and county levels. Nevertheless, I figured that since Central Park probably accounted for a huge share of New York County birding, the county list would provide a rough idea of my standing. By the way,

New York County and the borough of Manhattan are exactly the same place, to which I will refer by the latter name.

This list would soon dominate my thoughts and inspire an even more obsessive level of birding. Its creation was a bit of genius on the part of the developers of eBird, which requires a continuing supply of observations from thousands of birders in order to produce a useful, robust database. By providing some free recognition to those listing the most species, it encourages birders to contribute frequent, complete lists of what they observe. eBird is not explicitly staging a competition, but, if birders choose to see it that way, it can only benefit the cause of data-gathering.

I was delighted to learn that my 110 total would place me thirteenth among all Manhattan birders, not far outside the top ten—a good ranking for someone who had begun birding less than a year ago. I wanted my total to be known publicly, but this meant I would have to enter my birding records into eBird retroactively.

I had tried using eBird months before, after seeing an eBird user's daily list posted online. I got frustrated when it took me too long to enter a simple set of observations. (In retrospect the fault was mine, not eBird's—I did not realize that I could simply choose an area like "Central Park Ramble" and quickly check off the list of birds I saw in it rather than precisely pinpoint on a map the location of each sighting.)

eBird was touting an even newer, more streamlined entry process, so I wanted to try it again. It turned out to be easy and fast.

The only records I kept were of the date and location of each new species for the year, so my eBird lists were sparse, generally containing only one or two birds. It didn't matter—I carefully typed them in over the course of two days and eBird summed them up. Suddenly, in mid-September, my name appeared on the list of top New York County birders.

Being publicly ranked motivated me to bird harder and try to crack the top ten.

eBird also made me expand my birding range, since it counted observations made anywhere in Manhattan.

I had neglected birding in mid- to late August, and so had missed some species such as the Blue-winged Warbler, one of the early fall migrants.

Even worse, I did not bird areas outside of Central Park over the summer, which meant missing the peak shorebird season. Big mistake! I had missed the two shorebirds that typically appear in Central Park in the spring, Spotted Sandpiper and Solitary Sandpiper. It never occurred to me to look for them—my mind had been on warblers. I had also missed the several additional species—such as Killdeer, Semipalmated Sandpiper, and Greater Yellowlegs—that occur at Swindler Cove Park, Manhattan's top saltwater marsh.

I had also missed Laughing Gull, a species commonly seen any day of the summer on the East River and occasionally on the Reservoir.

Perhaps the most costly miss of all was not going to the Hudson or the East River for birds driven by Hurricane Irene on August 28. Expert birders were able to get as many as a dozen species that otherwise would rarely or never be observed in Manhattan. I did not yet view hurricanes as birding opportunities!

With these misses I was out of the running for a truly exceptional year, such as a top-five ranking, but the top ten was well within reach. From September 16–25, I added Great Blue Heron, Yellow-bellied Flycatcher, Veery, Yellow-billed Cuckoo, and Gray-cheeked Thrush to my 2011 list.

I discuss flycatchers and the Yellow-billed Cuckoo in Chapter 26.

The Veery and the Gray-cheeked both are thrushes. The former is much more common, roughly on par with the Wood

Thrush. If you do a few walks in the Ramble in May or September, you are likely to come across at least one Veery, which, like many other thrushes, often appears on the ground. The Gray-cheeked Thrush peaks a bit later, in mid-May and late September, and can be harder to identify because it resembles the much more common Swainson's Thrush but it has a pale, incomplete eye-ring (as opposed to the Swainson's buffy eye-ring with buffy spectacles). The key to observing the Gray-cheeked is timing: there is a week or so during both spring and fall migration when the species passes through in relatively large numbers, usually along with other thrushes. On the best days you might see five Gray-cheeked Thrushes along with dozens of Swainson's or Hermit Thrushes. Miss this period and you will have a very hard time finding any Gray-cheeked Thrushes.

Like the Wood Thrush, the Hermit Thrush is known for its beautiful, haunting song. It is a shame that Manhattan birders almost never get to hear it. The Hermit Thrush generally waits until it arrives at its breeding grounds far to the north before singing. Listen to some clips of it online and find out what you are missing.

You might, however, occasionally hear a Gray-cheeked Thrush singing in Manhattan. If you do, listen carefully, as there is a less well-known look-alike, the Bicknell's Thrush, which can be reliably distinguished from it only by voice. I have never positively observed one.

After entering all these birds, a tie for tenth place was mine! I was starting to think of myself as a competitive birder.

13

MR. OCTOBER

I put together a strategy for a big end-of-migration push. I would bird with Starr's group on Mondays and Wednesdays, starting in the Ramble at 7:30 a.m. On Tuesdays, Thursdays and Fridays I would begin with the American Museum of Natural History group at 7:00 a.m. Starr also did a North End walk on Tuesdays at 9:00 a.m., so I would run up to it after finishing my walk with the museum people.

I would also respond quickly to all online alerts, which I was having forwarded directly to my phone.

The result was a 23-bird month, a very strong showing that vaulted me into sixth place on the Manhattan top birders list.

I got many of the best birds on my own. Yellow-breasted Chat is a very rare songbird that is still classified as a warbler even though recent genetic research shows that it is more closely related to blackbirds and orioles. It is usually found on the ground or low in trees or brush, and it is well worth reporting. I saw one on a bush just east of the Maintenance Meadow men's room on October 2.

Philadelphia Vireo appeared on the same day in the Maintenance Meadow itself.

Blue Grosbeak is extremely rare throughout the New York City area and may be reported only a few times per year in Central Park. An online posting told of one being seen in the Wildflower Meadow near dusk on October 11. I arrived early the next morning to watch for it. After nearly an hour of waiting, I saw the female bird pop up to perch atop some of the tall vegetation in the field. Its thick bill easily distinguished it from the similar female Indigo Bunting.

I just happened to be wandering near the Reservoir in the late afternoon on the 18th when I saw photographers and birders intently viewing something on the water—a pair of Horned Grebes, a species seen in Central Park only several times per decade. This random encounter shows the value of actually being out in the park and observing, as no one reported these grebes online before darkness set in.

The month ended with an unusually early snowfall and the passage of a cold front. The heavy, wet snow falling on trees with leaves still in place caused tremendous damage in Central Park. Hundreds of trees were lost, and much of the Ramble would remain closed for over a month.

The conditions on the 30th were, however, very good for raptor migration, and I went to Riverside Park just below 92nd Street to observe it. I had learned from eBird observation history that the shore of the Hudson was a prime spot, and it did not disappoint. I had Snow Geese and over 40 Turkey Vultures.

The best bird came as I was finishing my session and exiting the park at 79th and Riverside Drive. I saw a very large, dark raptor gliding over the buildings of West End Avenue. It had distinct white patches near the ends of its primaries. It was a juvenile Golden Eagle!

This Golden Eagle would turn out to be my best bird of the year, and I was the only eBird user in Manhattan to report one in 2011. I was glad to have the added confirmation, though, that

14

WINTER VAGRANTS

The Varied Thrush from Chapter Four was my first experience with a vagrant, a bird that has wandered far from its regular habitat. Late 2011 brought several more to Manhattan.

First was the Rufous Hummingbird that appeared outside the West 81st Street entrance to the American Museum of Natural History on November 14. It was reported online at 3:05 p.m. and I wasted no time in running across the park to see it. When I arrived it was not being seen. I then made the mistake of giving up and running back after not quite 15 minutes. Later that evening I learned that it had reappeared before 4 p.m. and had been photographed.

Leaving the scene so quickly was a massive judgment error! Hummingbirds in mid-December have a hard time finding sustenance, as nectar-filled flowers are in short supply. This hummingbird was fortunate to find a flower-filled garden maintained by the museum, a life-saving oasis, as hummingbirds can die of starvation in as little as two hours. It would have to come back.

Up to then, Rufous Hummingbirds appeared in Central Park area rarely and irregularly—the last reported appearance of one there was in 2004. Why not wait at least until dark for a bird that might not come around for another seven years?

None of the other birders were leaving, so consider the implications: leaving means you definitely will not get the bird (at least not today) but those remaining might. Big year birders in competition with each other never want to be the first to leave.

That said, strategic errors do not always exact a toll. I returned early the next morning and saw the Rufous Hummingbird, species number 145 of 2011.

This bird attracted many viewers, and even earned a small article in the *New York Times*. I believe that it generated so much interest for two reasons: 1) it was the first widely-seen Rufous Hummingbird to appear in Manhattan in many years; 2) it chose a world-famous, easily accessible tourist destination as its roost.

Like the Varied Thrush, it stayed much longer than anyone expected. The museum put out a feeder for it, and it survived a mostly mild winter (with an arctic blast in early January) and was last observed in mid-March 2012.

A month later, on December 18, another rarity surfaced. Birders doing the annual Christmas Bird Count at Inwood Hill Park (at the northernmost tip of Manhattan) found a Dickcissel associating with a flock of House Sparrows on the Dyckman Street ball fields.

Dickcissels prefer grassland habitats and are native to the central plains states of the US, but some appear on the East Coast and, more specifically, in New York every year. They are very rare, however, in Manhattan.

Though I had never been to Inwood Hill Park before, getting the Dickcissel was easy once I arrived there. A large flock of House Sparrows was sallying out to the second baseball infield, near the backstop, and then flying back to the safety of a line of shrubs. After picking through 50 or so sparrows I saw the yellow eye-stripe and chest of the Dickcissel as the bird perched on a shrub.

While I was there, I wanted to visit nearby Swindler Cove Park to get the Orange-crowned Warbler that had been reported. This species had been appearing fairly frequently throughout the late fall in Central Park, but I never managed to get a glimpse of it there. My first effort at getting it in Swindler Cove Park also failed. I later learned from the birder who had found it that I had gone to the wrong part of the park. When I returned a few days later I got the bird nearly right away—number 148 of the year.

15

LAST BIRDS OF 2011

On the way back from Swindler Cove Park I stopped off near 140th Street on the West Side to look for the Monk Parakeets that had recently been sighted on the Hudson Greenway. These birds, of South American origin, have been breeding in New York City for roughly 40 years, and they long ago earned a spot on the American Birding Association's approved list, which prohibits such things as introduced birds or escaped pets until they have established enduring colonies.

Monk Parakeets are common in Queens and Brooklyn, but they were removed from Central Park in the 1970s as an invasive species and have been seen only fleetingly there since then. They recently had a well-known colony in Riverside Park and have been sighted more frequently in parts of Harlem.

They are loud, and I heard their grating squawks before I saw them perched on trees overlooking the Greenway. They were easy to find.

On December 30 I took a Staten Island Ferry ride in New York Harbor to see if I could increase my total with some waterfowl. Greater Scaup were abundant there, and with them I put my "little" big year of 2011 to rest at an even 150 species.

I finished sixth on the eBird New York County "Top Birders" list, just behind Richard Fried at 155. He broke the New York State Big Year record with 352 species in 2011, an even more impressive accomplishment when you consider that he continued his full-time work as a veterinarian.

I most certainly was not working full time anymore, though I was still trading nearly every day. I pondered the question of what to do as a new year was about to begin. I had focused intensely on school or work for all but a couple of the last thirty years, and I had the academic and professional achievements to show for it, along with a small measure of financial security. Taking it easy was an option.

But even if I could afford to spend a year doing nothing, this is not what I wanted. I felt mentally and physically sharp, rested and recovered after the stresses of the financial crisis that had started affecting my business as early as 2007 and which continued to require much maneuvering of personal investments until the middle of 2009. I had energy to expend, and I wanted to pour it into something worthwhile.

I considered getting back to active, short-term equity trading, but conditions had generally been poor for it in 2011—markets had mostly been stable, aside from a swift August selloff that failed to follow through. My equity trading techniques, much different from those I had used to manage mortgage hedge funds, worked better when the market experienced large, emotional swings, as it had during 2008. Longer-horizon investments had worked out well, but I did not need to sit in front of a screen and monitor them all day.

I had enjoyed my year of birding, and I felt fortunate that I got to spend so much time in the great parks of Manhattan, staying active and observing nature. Not everyone can just decide to cut out of work when the warblers are passing through.

In addition, I relished the mental stimulation that birding provided. Viewing intently, listening carefully, and constantly analyzing patterns of shape, color, and sound gave my brain a satisfying workout.

I also was proud to have achieved a level of competence, though certainly not yet excellence, after taking my first birding walk little more than a year before. I did not want to stop birding, but on the other hand I was not sure I wanted to continue approaching it with the same competitive zeal.

I should mention that amassing a high annual species total does not necessarily indicate a high level of birding skill. Big years are, to a great extent, logistical challenges, particularly when they take place over large geographic areas. They reward those with the time to travel and bird every day or, at the very least, those who can chase rarities at a moment's notice. There is more to birding than just observing a great many species at least once!

Nevertheless, big years are immensely challenging, and birding skills prove highly advantageous to those doing them. Big years (along with lifetime lists) are the most prominent and popular forms of competition among birders. They may not be great measures of birding achievement, but they are the measures that we have.

16

RUSH TO GET THE RARITIES

I felt ambivalent about trying for another big year. The argument in favor: I could see myself doing a lot better, maybe even 25 birds better, than the 150 with which I would close 2011. The argument against: it would require an enormous amount of time, at least three hours a day on 80% of the days of the year, and I would have to struggle to finish any better than fifth. The top birders were that good.

Andrew Farnsworth was one of the most skilled birders in the nation, a member of the national champion Sapsucker big-day team from Cornell University. He had turned his midtown apartment, with a close view of the East River's migration pathway, into a high-tech birding laboratory complete with powerful scopes, sound sensors, and software to identify birds by flight calls, the subject of his PhD thesis in ornithology. Since 2008 he had reported the highest species totals among Manhattan birders on eBird every year. His 2011 total, boosted by a trove of hurricane birds, was 221.

Jacob Drucker, who finished in second place with 183 birds, was a brilliant collegiate birder with over eight years experience. He frequently posted his daily lists online, often with large species counts and many rarities. He was reputed to possess unusually sharp visual and auditory birding skills. He achieved his Manhattan total despite being away at college in Massachusetts for most of the year, returning only for quick weekend forays and during school vacations.

Stephen Chang, who finished in third place with 177 birds, was a highly-respected, experienced birder who submitted the most Manhattan eBird checklists of anyone in 2011—more than one per day, on average. His reports revealed a precise, meticulous approach to identifying birds, and he had contributed to *The Kingbird*, a publication of the New York State Ornithological Association.

I did not know much about Anders Peltomaa, who finished in fourth place with 166 birds, except that he birded frequently, posted results online often and intelligently, and was willing to visit distant parks to get rare birds. He also had a very strong fall 2011 season, maintaining his lead over me despite starting from a much higher total.

At the time I had no idea if these birders, or any of the other top birders (aside from Richard Fried, at the state level), had specifically been trying to have "big years," i.e., trying to maximize their annual species totals, and I certainly did not know their plans for 2012. Still, the top three birders from 2011 had also finished in exactly the same order in 2010. So, whether they achieved their high totals on purpose or as a natural consequence of being prolific and perceptive birders, it did not matter; they appeared to be consistent, and they would likely put up similar numbers in 2012. To contend with them, I would need to take my birding to a much higher level.

It is worth pointing out here that not all birders report their observations on eBird. Starr Saphir, for example, does not (until August 2012 she had no computer) and her Manhattan totals would have ranked her among the top five as long as eBird has been in existence. I have no doubt that there are others, too, who see many species but who do not report them publicly. Of course, there is no way for me to write about these people. Among its many useful features, eBird provides a great scoreboard for birding competition, free and visible to all. Many of Manhattan's best birders, particularly those who want their results to be widely known and available for scientific study, do use it; they are the ones who appear in this book.

I settled on this plan: bird aggressively to start the year and see how well I could do before committing to a year-long pursuit. For most birders, January in New York is not the time to expend unusual effort. I thought I had a good chance of finally cracking the top five or better. Migrants do not start appearing until mid-March, so I would not need a staggering total to maintain a high rank during the winter months.

First priority was re-observing the rare vagrants that I had just gotten in December: Rufous Hummingbird, Dickcissel, and Orange-crowned Warbler. These birds could move or die at any time, and the odds of getting one later in the year were poor.

In addition, Bryant Park in midtown was hosting some birds that I had already had in 2011 but that I needed for 2012: Ovenbird, Gray Catbird, Lincoln's Sparrow and Yellow-breasted Chat. The first two would be very easy to get later in the spring; the latter two were rare and well worth getting now.

January 1, 2012, began sunny and warm, with an expected high in the low 50s—a great day for birding. I did not want cold weather to drive out or imperil the vagrants.

I had only the morning free to bird, so I would not have time to get the Dickcissel at Inwood. Instead I went directly across Central Park, picking up a Yellow-bellied Sapsucker on the way, to the American Museum of Natural History to see the most fragile of the vagrants, the Rufous Hummingbird. I found it quickly; it was alive and well, living off of the sugar-water provided for it.

Then I took the subway to Bryant Park. The Gray Catbird and the Ovenbirds showed up right away, but the two birds I most wanted did not appear at all, despite over an hour of searching. I had to end my birding early, before 11:30, to get ready for lunch with my girlfriend. I would not be putting up any decent numbers today.

Meanwhile, Farnsworth was having an epic day, visiting the same four parks on my itinerary and getting the rare vagrants along with the Bryant Park birds. He additionally had Killdeer, Black-crowned Night-Heron, and Cedar Waxwing (all at Swindler Cove), along with 36 common species in Central Park. These impressive results, and the date on which they occurred, left no doubt: Farnsworth cared about annual totals and intended to defend his ranking as Manhattan's top birder.

I knew I had to get as many birds as possible on Monday the Second, as it would be the last warm day before sub-freezing weather arrived.

Starting a bit late at 10:15 a.m., I ran along the Reservoir and picked up the usual, common waterfowl on my way to the subway, where a 40-minute ride would take me to Inwood Hill Park.

It took me longer to find the Dickcissel this time, close to an hour, but I got it. Then I went directly to Swindler Cove Park and got the Orange-crowned Warbler quickly, as it was chipping from a tree in front of the mud flats, along with a bird Farnsworth had not gotten: Great Blue Heron. I was done with Swindler by 2 p.m. — early enough for the one-hour trek back to Bryant Park.

I searched Bryant Park thoroughly but was unable to find either the Yellow-breasted Chat or the Lincoln's Sparrow. After six miles of walking and two hours on the subway, the sun was going down and it was time to go home. A full day of effort had rewarded me with fewer birds than I had hoped.

I wish I had been able to bird more on Sunday. The cold air arrived on Tuesday the Third, and it surely suppressed bird activity. I went to Central Park to stock up on the more common species that I had put off getting, and things went just OK. I did the Reservoir and Ramble in the morning, and southern Central Park in the afternoon.

I was happy to get the Red-headed Woodpecker that had been hanging out in Hallet Sanctuary. It was not a vagrant but a rare species for the area well worth getting. In both of the past two winters, a juvenile Red-headed Woodpecker had taken up residence in southern Central Park.

Meanwhile, I had been following the situation at Bryant Park via online postings, and I learned that the Yellow-breasted Chat was being seen on the park's eastern (Fifth Avenue) side, which contains the entrance to the New York Public Library.

So on Wednesday the Fourth, which would turn out to be the coldest day of the year (it was 17° F when I arrived), I finally added the Yellow-breasted Chat. It was hopping around the planters just a few feet from me on the northeast side of the library—a neotropical migrant that really ought to be roaming the warm, woodsy thickets of Guatemala by now instead of wandering the cold, gravel-filled hedges of midtown Manhattan. I am just glad I got it, as the other chat had been found dead aside the ice-skating rink the previous day.

As for the Lincoln's Sparrow, none of the many reputable birders who tried were able to find it in January at Bryant Park.

Later in the day I ran along the East River in the 96th–107th Street area and added two key waterfowl, Red-breasted Merganser and Red-throated Loon. These are common, expected species on the East River (and the Hudson, too) in January, but those who bird only Central Park are not certain to get the former and probably will miss the latter.

On Thursday the Fifth I went for a Staten Island Ferry ride to get some New York Harbor waterfowl. I added Greater Scaup, which is tough to get on the two rivers, and Brant, which is easy to get on them—but another bird that you will almost never find on Central Park waters.

Then I went to nearby Battery Park for what I considered one of my smarter plays, getting the famous resident Wild Turkey, Zelda, who had lived there since 2003.

Wild Turkeys no longer wander into Manhattan with any regularity, though there is always a slim chance of coming across one in Inwood Hill Park, which borders the Bronx. I did not want to take any chances at missing Zelda, as she was probably at least ten years old, which is frightfully old for her species. Most Wild Turkeys never make it past two in the wild (they are easy prey), and in captivity 13 years appears to be the maximum.

As a postscript, I am happy to report that Zelda not only survived Hurricane Sandy, whose 100+ mph winds and extreme flooding devastated the Battery Park area, but also the entire year. She was still strutting about the Battery Park playground in early 2013.

A quick trip to the Compost Heap area in Central Park on the Sixth gave me two more birds including a Chipping Sparrow, unusual for this time of year but easy to get later in the spring.

I was now, after six days into 2012, feeling much better about my nascent big year. Farnsworth had tallied an amazing 65 birds. I was right behind him in second place with 54. Jacob Drucker was third with 52. I had achieved my goal of nabbing a medal spot. Could I hang on?

17

JANUARY BIRDING MANIA

If your goal is simply to have a big year in Manhattan, once you have gotten the vagrants, the lingering rarities, the seasonal waterfowl, and the usual common birds—all of which you can do in a week or two—you can take a long break and wait to chase new rare bird reports.

My goal also was to put up big numbers right now in January, and that meant I had to keep birding.

Many birds that pop up in January are much easier to get later in the year. For example, early in the month Nashville Warbler and Black-throated Green Warbler were seen at Inwood Hill Park. Listing them now would gain me no long-term advantage—any serious birder would certainly see these species, likely often, during spring migration. It didn't matter—I wanted to list them now!

I also wanted to try for the Swindler Cove Killdeer that other birders had been reporting. Killdeer is likely, but by no means a sure thing, during the Manhattan summer shorebird season. Going for *this* bird actually made sense.

Another bird that made sense to pursue now was Great Horned Owl. One had been observed since late December in the pines of Inwood Hill. The problem was that I had only vague information regarding where to look.

So, late on the morning of Sunday, January 8, I made an hour-long trek to Inwood Hill Park.

I searched the Dyckman ball field area for the Nashville and did not see it. I walked further north to the elevated passage over the train tracks and proceeded into the forested area of the park, where the Black-throated Green was seen. I did not see it, either. Then I walked the trails for about a half-mile, hoping to hear some Blue Jays mobbing the owl—this is how others had discovered it. I did not hear any.

In fact, I was not hearing much of anything. The interior of the park seemed to have long stretches of lifelessness—tall, bare trees standing close together with no birds to be seen or heard.

This was the first time I had been inside the Inwood Hill forest, and I found it eerie, too isolated even for me. Central Park had some small patches like it, but, in general, one there is never much more than 100 yards from a busy running path, road, or clearing.

Inwood Hill Park is much different. It truly is on a hill and a tall, steep one at that. You quickly climb 150–200 feet to get on the trails. Instead of being in the middle of a dense, urban area, it is bounded by water on the west and north sides. A quiet neighborhood lies to the south. The park gets very little foot traffic compared to Central Park. Moreover, much of the park leaves the visitor a half-mile from civilization and hundreds of feet above the surrounding area.

Inwood Hill and adjacent Isham Park had two violent incidents in December 2011, which is high relative to the number of visitors these parks get. Central Park, by contrast, has only become safer over the years. Many factors have been behind this improvement, including more active policing, a citywide decline in crime, and less isolation within the park—according to a Central Park Conservancy report, usage has nearly tripled since 1982. Even birds know that there is safety in numbers.

I do not want to discourage people from visiting Inwood Hill Park, which is well worth seeing not just for the birds one can observe here but for its own natural beauty. During daylight hours, the Dyckman ball fields and the area around the eastern saltmarsh get plenty of park goers along with frequent police coverage, and they always feel safe. If you want to go deeper into the park's forest, you may want to go with a friend or join one of the free ranger-led birding walks.

I was glad to make it to the southern end of the park where sparrows and titmice again appeared along with dog walkers and hikers.

From there it is a fifteen-minute walk, mostly east on Dyckman, to Swinder Cove Park, which is largely a salt marsh with surrounding dry land. This time it did not produce even a single new bird. No Killdeer, no Black-crowned Night-Heron, and not even a simple Golden-crowned Kinglet, as had been reported recently.

I walked back to the Dyckman area of Inwood Hill to try one more time for the warblers or perhaps an American Tree Sparrow, which Jacob Drucker had reported hearing on his recent visit. Again, I had no luck.

I figured I would give Swindler Cove one more try, and I retraced my steps back to it. Still nothing!

It was around 3 p.m., and I did not want to bird all day without adding at least one species. So I took the subway back downtown, stopping off on the Upper West Side at 145th Street and heading to the Hudson Greenway to re-find some Monk Parakeets.

The trees on which they had been feeding in November were now bare, and there were no parakeets to be found.

I saw just one remaining option: head one mile south to Riverside Church and see one of its resident Peregrine Falcons. I ran there and was finally rewarded with the only new species of the day and number 55 of the year.

By the time I got back home I figured I had walked or run over ten miles. Was I really thinking of doing this sort of thing *all year long*?

Apparently so, as two days later I was once again on my way to Swindler Cove Park. This time I would have more to show for it: a Belted Kingfisher (a bird that can be tough to get in Central Park, even during migration) and a Hermit Thrush.

As I was walking along Dyckman Street on my way to Inwood Hill, I saw an American Kestrel fly over and perch on a nearby building. Score! I tried for the warblers and the American Tree Sparrow again but missed. Still, I was pleased to add three birds.

Back to Central Park on January 12, I found the Eastern Phoebe that was trying to winter in the Gill area of the Ramble. What I wanted in addition to it was a Brown Creeper, a relatively common bird seen crawling up trees during the winter and even more frequently during the spring. I recall several hours wandering the Ramble that day and the following day, scanning trees for a tiny brown bird. Naturally, once I found one I found another just minutes later.

Manhattan has a number of tiny parks that sometimes hold wintering birds. Bryant Park, mentioned earlier, is one of them. Another is Union Square Park. These parks are surrounded by urban development, and I suspect that birds in them see no evidence that flying out would take them to better habitat on the amount of energy they have left, so they stay put.

Union Square Park had reports of three good birds: Yellow-breasted Chat (which I had already listed), Swamp Sparrow, and White-crowned Sparrow. When I went there on the 16th I could find only the first two.

Over the next few days Central Park produced Red-winged

Blackbird (common) and Brown-headed Cowbird (uncommon, though not rare, and fairly easy to get in the spring).

Saturday, January 21, became a memorable birding day for two reasons: the city received its first blanket of snow since the late-October storm, and I added a bird indoors! Someone had recently reported on eBird seeing a variety of birds at the public atrium at 590 Madison Avenue. They were birds of wild origin that enjoyed year-round warmth, ample flying space (ceiling height over 40 feet), access to well-maintained vegetation areas, and food—from atrium diners, seed put out for them, and insects. The birds included two Gray Catbirds, a Dark-eyed Junco, and the one that I needed: Brown Thrasher[1].

By month's end, my walks in Central Park had added Northern Flicker and Black-capped Chickadee. The latter was very hard to find this winter after having been abundant at the feeders the previous two winters.

My 66th bird tied me for first place in the eBird standings with Jacob Drucker. Andrew Farnsworth was one bird behind, and the others were at least 18 birds back of him.

I knew, however, that my large lead on the rest of the field was mostly meaningless. Though I had picked up a few very hard birds that others had neglected to pursue (e.g., the Dickcissel and the Orange-crowned Warbler), nearly all of my lead was built on relatively common birds that people were almost sure to get later in the year. If I wanted to maintain my lead, I would have to work even harder and get some rare birds that others were unlikely to get.

---

[1] Some may argue that this bird was captive, with the atrium serving as a large "cage," and hence ineligible for listing according to ABA rules. My response: *I* had no problem finding a means of egress, and I listed many other Brown Thrashers in the park later in the year!

18

GETTING THE TOUGH BIRDS

I did not have to wait long to have a shot at some rare birds. On the afternoon of February 2, a report was posted online of a Redhead duck and some Lesser Scaup near Pier 11 downtown on New York Harbor. I immediately put on my coat and took the subway to Wall Street, and from there I ran to Pier 11. I arrived on the scene within 45 minutes of the report. I did not see any other birders, but the male Redhead and the small flock of Lesser Scaup were floating a mere 30 feet offshore in a sheltered bay between piers.

Both of these species turned out to be crucial, as none of the other top ten birders on the year would get either of them. I was thankful for the birder who found and reported them, and glad that I wasted no time in going to get them. I knew from the previous year's results that sightings at the extremes of Manhattan—the Inwood area on the north and the harbor on the south—were particularly valuable because most other birders would not bother to chase them. It was hard to build a lead with just birds from Central Park, as rarities reported there usually end up being seen by many of the more serious birders.

Building on this idea, two days later—on Saturday, February 4—

I took a long run, with binoculars in hand, up the Hudson River as far as 145th Street. On the way I saw three swimming Mute Swans. This species can be very hard to get in Manhattan or very easy, depending on whether or not a swan decides to linger on Central Park waters such as the Meer. Only Farnsworth had seen one so far this year, so I considered it a great find.

The object of my run was Canvasback, which had been sighted on the Hudson recently in this area. I did not see any, nor did I see any Monk Parakeets at their usual hangout by the Greenway.

On the way back through Riverside Park, I stopped when I heard a high whistling. It was my first-of–year Golden-crowned Kinglet, an easy bird during migration but one that I had wanted ever since I missed it at Swindler Cove. Two birds on the day put me at an even 70 for the year.

Since New York Harbor had been good to me earlier, I went there again on Sunday, February 5, and added two excellent birds: Great Cormorant, which is fairly common there and on the two rivers; and Horned Grebe, which is much less common. Best of all, neither bird is likely to appear in Central Park—though in 2012 both defied long odds and showed up on the Reservoir.

On the way back from the harbor I stopped off at Union Square Park. I had recently tried this location twice, and though I had seen two of the reported birds—yet another wintering Yellow-breasted Chat and a Swamp Sparrow—I had missed the adult White-crowned Sparrow, a bird I very much wanted to get. It showed up every year in both spring and fall migration, but never in large numbers. In general, it was harder to get than Swamp Sparrow but easier than Lincoln's Sparrow.

I had no idea how it was eluding me in such a tiny park, where it had been reported to range over an area roughly that of a basketball half-court. Taking a few steps farther so that I could view the north side of a hedgerow finally put my quarry in view.

What a bright white crown! This aptly-named bird entered my list at number 73.

I then remained stuck at that total for another three weeks. February can be an unrewarding month to bird Manhattan, particularly if you birded actively in January. There is no new migration, and the bird population of Central Park seems to decline in both variety and total numbers—outflow without inflow.

It seemed like a good time to redirect my attention to the Great Horned Owl residing in Inwood Hill Park. This owl was being reported on a little-followed online forum called "InwoodBirdwatchers." Apparently its roosting location was well-known to the regulars of Inwood Hill Park. At least one birder gave directions to the roost, which I did not find explicit enough to follow. Several birders posted Flickr photos of the owl and the unusual hanging tree branch near it, and these, however, turned out to be the key to finding it. The photos had GPS coordinates associated with them, and it was easy to plot the collection of them on Google maps. I was glad to see that they all fell within a small area, suggesting that the coordinates were credible. The owl appeared to be close to the eastern edge of the park.

I studied the photos for all possible visual cues: the distinctive hanging branch, the direction of sunlight, the curve in the dirt path, and the wooden beams lining the path. On Sunday, February 26, I was ready to go. It was warm and sunny with little wind—fine conditions for birding. I appeared to have a choice of paths into the park from my decided entry point. The first led me too far into the park to be the right one. I retraced my steps and took the other path. The wooden beams lining it added to my confidence, and soon I saw the broken branch hanging upside-down. Close to the branch was a large blob with a reddish face and ear tufts: I had found the Great Horned Owl! It was huge, and it had the fierce look of a top predator, which it was.

It was another excellent bird for Manhattan, one not seen every year in Central Park. No one else had listed it on eBird for the county, so for now I was another bird up on the entire field.

After taking some time to admire it, I followed the path back out to the eastern ball fields, where I had entered. I still had some birding to do. Hairy Woodpecker had been reported in the Inwood area recently, and Inwood Hill Park was known to host this species. So, for that matter, did Central Park, but I was not seeing any there.

I checked the Dyckman ball field area for warblers, which by now probably were long gone. As I was walking back toward the subway on Dyckman Street, I kept an eye on the park's tree-filled grassy slope. Soon I saw a large black and white woodpecker whose long, thick bill confirmed my initial guess: it was the Hairy Woodpecker.

The two species added today brought my total for the year to 75, and this is where I would finish the month. Andrew Farnsworth was right behind with 70, followed by Jacob Drucker at 66 (he had not birded Manhattan at all in February), then Anders Peltomaa in fourth at 56.

I was glad to pick up five very hard birds in February. My early lead now had some substance.

19

BIRDING BY EAR

Starr Saphir and Stephen Quinn had demonstrated the power of birding by ear, and I wanted to have that power working for me.

Birding by ear is a practical skill for the big year birder to have; it can save you much time and effort, and, with the resources available on the internet to aid in learning it, there is no excuse not to have a least a rudimentary grasp of it. Some essential birds, such as certain flycatchers, can *only* be authoritatively identified in the field by a combination of plumage and song. Apart from its pragmatic benefits, learning bird calls and songs adds another dimension to the birding experience, helping you to be more aware of what is going on around you.

Winter is an excellent time to acquire this skill as it is most needed during spring migration, when the woods come alive with bird song. One generally is not birding too much in the late-January to early-March period, leaving more time for study.

I had already learned the sounds of the commonest birds, the ones that spend most of the year in Central Park. I needed to work harder on the migrants: the warblers, orioles, tanagers, vireos and flycatchers that move through the park each spring and fall.

To organize my learning, I decided to make a spreadsheet. I

listed all the birds that I expected to be around during spring migration with separate rows for "songs" (the most complex, extended vocalizations, often used to attract a mate) and "calls" (shorter, simpler, less lyrical, and often louder than songs). It is generally the male that sings (there are exceptions), but both sexes may emit calls, which I take to include chip notes.

Ducks, hawks, and gulls are identified almost always just by sight, so I did not include these groups.

Birders describe bird calls and songs with a sort of shorthand: syllables and phrases that we humans can say. So, for example, my spreadsheet had the lines:

Yellow Warbler, Song: *"sweet-sweet-sweet-I'm-so-sweet"* (accelerating, whistled);
Yellow Warbler, Call: *"chip"*

In order for the above to be useful, you first need to have heard the actual song and call. The shorthand provides a mnemonic that will help you recall the sounds. It should also work in reverse: when you hear the bird song, you are reminded of the shorthand, which you have associated with the species. After much listening in the field you find that you can go directly from species to sound and back.

To hear bird sounds on your computer, you have a number of options. The Cornell site *AllAboutBirds* is an excellent starting point. It has photos, descriptions, and sound clips for nearly all the species that occur in the United States. The sound clips usually come with commonly-used mnemonics in the associated text. You can find an even larger collection of sound clips at the online McCaulay Library.

I used these clips (and those from other sources) to record my own mp3 files, which I then imported into iTunes playlists. Since these were purely for my personal use, making digital copies was all right.

The result was a free library of bird sounds on which I could drill. I worked both ways: going down the list of species names and imagining their sounds, and listening to the songs (sometimes in shuffled order) and trying to identify the species.

If you have a smartphone or recent-model iPod, you can save yourself the work of making mp3 files. There are a number of reasonably-priced apps that integrate photos and sound files for nearly all North American birds.

I began drilling in February and by the time the first warblers started arriving, in March, I had a decent grasp of many primary songs and calls—a very basic foundation on which to build.

A month of studying tapes will no more make you an expert at bird sounds than will a month of intensive French make you a fluent Francophone. Birds are amazingly nuanced communicators. Most have more than one call. They have flight calls, contact calls, begging calls (from nestlings), threat calls, and alarm calls, for example. They may slightly improvise their songs or sing only parts of a song. On the tapes, you usually hear only a single species vocalizing a single call or song against a quiet background. In the field, you more frequently hear a jumble of bird sounds coming from many species. Learning to pick out and focus on the lines that are most important to you takes much practice. Migration season would provide plenty of opportunity for me to refine my skills.

20

BIRD BLOGGING

Back in October I told Starr she ought to have a website to better advertise her walks. New York City Audubon, with whom she was affiliated, promoted her as one of their birding tour guides and also displayed her schedule as part of their activities calendar. Other than this, Starr lacked an internet presence, and I believed that this was hurting her business.

Starr did not even have a computer, nor did her co-leader, Lenore Swenson. I encouraged Starr to get one, which I knew she would find useful as she had a wide variety of interests, but fitting one into her budget was difficult. By late March I realized that I would need to take action on my own.

I suggested to Starr that I would create a personal website for her. It would not cost her—or me—anything, and it would advertise her walks and help her attract more people to them. It would be more than just an electronic billboard, though; it would attract viewers with birding-related content that they could not get anywhere else via a blog that she and I would write.

I proposed doing something that no other Central Park birding guide was doing: providing complete reports of every walk, with lists of species observed and informative commentary, and posting these reports quickly, well before the day was over. People who had gone on the walks could review what they had just seen and reinforce their learning.

Starr was excited about the idea, and wanted to name the site *StarrTrips*, after her personal tour-giving company. I should have known what bird she would want featured above the text of her site: the Cerulean Warbler, of course!

Starr had another good reason to want to promote herself online. I had learned through my own internet searching that she was the featured subject of a documentary film, produced by local birder Jeffrey Kimball, called *Birders: The Central Park Effect*, which would be broadcast on HBO over the summer. She was about to become even more famous.

I made sure that everything on her site was in order before mentioning it on the online message board eBirdsNYC, which was popular with New York City birders.

Posting the results of the more successful walks to the boards quickly, usually within an hour of the walk's end, and including a link to her site became standard procedure during spring migration. Starr was doing what she had always done—finding rare birds and racking up impressive daily species totals—but suddenly more people knew about it.

Starr left a phone message for me most Thursdays with her review of the week's birding. I transcribed the message and posted it on her site. I wrote the daily summaries on my own. The blog was well received among Central Park birders, and the satisfaction I gained from creating it surely encouraged me to write this book.

Better yet, the website and blog helped to attract more people to Starr's walks.

21

BLACK VULTURE

Eastern Towhees are easy birds to get in Central Park if you wait for their peak migration in mid-April. You will hear them all over the Ramble, the males singing *"drink-your-tea!"* and both sexes calling *"tow-hee,"* which is how they got the name.

I did not want to wait—I wanted one now. Several had been reported in the Ramble since January. When I went to where one had been seen, around Belvedere Castle, I never saw it. Starting in mid-February one was reported at the Swedish Cottage, so I made a point of passing by the Cottage often in hopes of catching a glimpse. I did not see it.

In early March I was searching the area just west of Shakespeare Garden when I finally spotted this elusive male Eastern Towhee. As I looked at the wooden building just beyond it, I realized *this* was the Swedish Cottage! How could I have forgotten? I had even been inside the Cottage once for a social event involving a Swedish family. What I had been searching in the Ramble was another much less developed wooden structure known as the Rustic Shelter. Moral: do not confuse the birding locations, and do not get so worked up about common birds.

One other common bird had been giving me fits: Winter Wren, a tiny, mouse-like bird almost always seen scurrying over muddy shorelines and around rotting wood. Its song is softer than that of the other two wrens common to Central Park—Carolina and House—and it is also somewhat harder to observe. I had completely missed it in January. As of March 8, one began to be sighted in the Loch of Central Park's North End. I could have waited for a better time in migration, but if others could see it, I also ought to be able to see it! I was not about to back down from the challenge. It took me several visits before I finally saw it, on March 18, moving along the shore.

I had a similar experience with Rusty Blackbird, an uncommon bird for Central Park. One had been reported around the Ramble in January and February, but I never saw it. It is a tough bird to find for two reasons: first, there are not very many of them. It has experienced, as a species, one of the largest population declines, possibly as much as 90% over 40 years, and there may be only two or three in the entire park even at peak times of the year. Second, it superficially resembles Common Grackle, of which there *are* plenty. It does not tend to mix with other birds, though, so the key is to look for a lone blackbird, usually in a swampy area like the Gill or the Loch, and then confirm field marks. I found one in the Loch on March 28.

What about warblers? The Pine Warblers arrived early in 2012, on March 10. On the next day I went to the exact pine tree in Nutter's Battery where one had been reported and saw it.

I thought that other warblers might also follow the example and arrive early, but they did not. Palm Warbler arrived on the 29th, and I saw it then.

It was a lackluster month, partly because I had already gotten the winter birds and at least one typical March arrival, Eastern Phoebe, earlier. I added only ten birds, bringing my year's total to 85. My lead, however, grew, with Andrew Farnsworth at 74 and Anders Peltomaa at 68. Jacob Drucker, who did not bird Manhattan in March, remained at 66.

I did have one standout species, however: I saw a pair of Black Vultures gliding over the Lake on the 29th. This species has only a few eBird records in Manhattan prior to 2012. Mine was the only report of this species in Central Park in all of 2012.

Turkey Vultures, by contrast, are fairly common flyover birds in the spring and fall, and I also had these on the 26th.

Both vultures, along with hawks and eagles, are diurnal migrants—meaning they migrate during the day, when they can catch a ride on rising air currents and then conserve energy by gliding.

It is odd that Black Vultures are seen frequently just north of Manhattan in Westchester County, in places such as Bedford and Ossining, but rarely in Manhattan itself. From looking at an eBird map of historical sightings it becomes clear that most Black Vultures passing through Westchester must either be following the Hudson River south or crossing directly over it and moving south through New Jersey.

Manhattan birders wishing to see a Black Vulture can put the odds in their favor by visiting Fort Tryon Park or the Dyckman baseball fields of Inwood Hill Park during October or November and looking across the Hudson River. Since the river is roughly a mile wide, a spotting scope may be helpful. Black Vultures along with other large birds that are difficult to observe in Manhattan, Common Ravens, may be seen over New Jersey's Palisades Park to the west. Occasionally they fly across the river to the New York side, allowing the viewer to get them according to strict ABA recording rules, which require "that the bird be in the prescribed area when observed, though the observer need not be." Sticklers may note that the middle of the Hudson River is the exact dividing line between New York and New Jersey.

22

RADAR, METEOROLOGY, AND BIRDING

Most passerines, including warblers, migrate at night. I learned from Andrew Farnsworth a high-tech way to observe and measure bird migration without ever going outside: radar!

The radar maps you see on many popular weather sites may not, however, do the job. Some sites and smart phone apps filter radar data so that only very strong echoes, such as those caused by precipitation, are displayed. You need to visit sites and use apps that do not filter radar data, such as the National Weather Service weather.gov site or RadarScope.

If visiting the weather.gov site, find the radar that covers your local area. Select the loop with "base reflectivity," and click the display to focus on your desired location. If you want to see whether nocturnal migration is occurring where you are, you will want to log on at least 30-45 minutes after sunset. The colored areas of movement that you see are most likely birds, bats, and insects in flight, with denser concentrations producing more intense echoes. The map's legend matches echo color with intensity, as measured in dBZ. A search for Dr. Sid Gauthreaux's calibration curve that relates this type of radar data with direct visual observations will help you do the math to figure out approximately how dense a movement is occurring. Also, there is a great deal of information online about how to distinguish birds from insects and bats, although this can be challenging. The important thing is to remember, when looking only at reflectivity during intense spring and fall movement periods, that you will be seeing birds, bats, and insects!

At times throughout the year, Farnsworth would alert local birders to unusually good overnight migration from his monitoring of radar, advising them to look for new migrants in the park the following morning. This advice generally proved worthwhile. Sometimes he would advise not to even wait for the morning—just go outside, look, and listen. If cloud cover is low, many passerines may fly low enough to be illuminated and made visible by the lights of tall city structures.

Farnsworth has gotten dozens of species from visual night birding. Some have come from right outside his window, where neighboring buildings have lights shining up. The light is not strong enough for him to identify plumage colors, but he can discern overall shape, a key element of bird identification. This allows him to identify birds with unusual shapes. He often gets American Woodcock this way, a rounded bird with a very long bill. Other species that stand out are Northern Flicker, Peregrine Falcon, American Kestrel, and the cuckoos (though the Black-billed is indistinguishable from the Yellow-billed based only on shape).

Other species have come from watching the Empire State Building, a structure tall enough to shine on the flight paths of many birds.

Many have come from an event unique to New York, the *Tribute in Light,* a memorial to victims of the September 11, 2001, attacks. At this annual event many powerful searchlights are focused to create two intense beams shining directly upward. Thousands of migrating birds become trapped in these beams, which have to be turned off occasionally to allow the birds to reorient themselves and escape. Farnsworth often monitors the beams and has identified over 40 species in them. You can get an idea of the incredible volume of overnight fall migration by searching YouTube for videos of *Tribute in Light* birds.

Birds may also, regardless of cloud cover, fly low enough to be heard. Farnsworth's area of expertise is flight calls, and he regularly detects a great variety of species migrating overhead at night with listening equipment he has built into his high-rise apartment. If you go to a high spot, such as Belvedere Castle, in Central Park at night during a migration season and it is quiet, you may be able to hear these calls with ears alone; this is particularly true on nights with fog or low cloud ceiling. Farnsworth led a large group in October 2012 from the Linnaean Society of New York there for just this purpose.

Birders can also benefit from monitoring the winds and the movement of weather fronts. It's simple: birds want fly north in the spring and south in the fall. They need to use their limited supplies of energy wisely or they will weaken and possibly perish. This means they prefer to fly with the wind at their backs. When winds switch to being favorable after many unfavorable nights, you can expect that there will be pent-up demand for migration and that more birds will take advantage of the good conditions. These are the mornings you want to be birding.

Wind also plays a strong role in bird vagrancy. The most extreme example is hurricane-related vagrancy, and I discuss this topic in Chapter 36. Why some birds make migration errors is not fully understood, but strong, persistent winds of lesser intensity also can facilitate the wanderings of such birds. Even birds not actively choosing errant migration paths can be blown off course enough that they have no choice but to follow the wind and make a long voyage well outside their normal range. A powerful low pressure system in the North Atlantic can create strong northeast winds that push European species out to sea and on course for North America. Vagrants from Europe include

Barnacle Goose, Eurasian Wigeon, Lesser Black-backed Gull, Fieldfare, and Northern Lapwing. Pressure system configurations that cause strong westerly winds, particularly during fall migration, can deliver more vagrants of western origin, such as Cave Swallow, Ash-throated Flycatcher, and Black-throated Gray Warbler, to the eastern United States. The best way to stay informed about likely vagrants and meteorological effects on birds in general is to follow the *BirdCast* site, which offers the latest research and forecasts.

Temperature also plays an important role in signaling when to migrate. It is no secret that average temperatures have been rising during recent decades. Many bird species have responded to this change by migrating earlier in the spring, a fact demonstrated both scientifically[1] and anecdotally, with spring temperature playing the most important role. Case in point: the winter and spring of 2012 turned out to be among the warmest of all time in the United States and many migrants appeared even earlier than their "new normal" times.

Warmer climate has also pushed forward the times at which flowers bloom and insects hatch. Birds that migrate early can thus take advantage of more available food, but what about those birds that have less flexible schedules, or that rely less on temperature as a cue? Long-distance migrants appear to alter their migration timing less than those species traveling shorter distances. A study using tracking devices showed that individual Wood Thrushes repeated their spring migration departures from Central America and breeding ground arrivals in southern Canada with only a day or two of variation from year to year. Those species less able to adapt may find their numbers further imperiled.

---

[1] One of many studies demonstrating this was done using eBird data: Hurlbert and Liang, 2012, *Spatiotemporal Variation in Avian Migration Phenology*.

Long-distance migrants face another problem: they need to find food at all stopover points along the way. Yet northern climates are changing more than temperate ones and much more than tropical ones. A schedule that is timed optimally for the ultimate destination does no good if it leads to starvation along the way.

Many species also migrate to different locations than they used to. A 2009 Audubon Society study showed that over half of the 305 bird species tracked were spending their summers an average of 35 miles farther north than they did 40 years ago.

The effects of climate on fall migration are more complicated and less uniform among species, and they partly depend on whether a species raises single or multiple summer broods.

One thing is generally true, however: cold weather in the fall encourages birds to migrate south. The combination of a cold front passing though along with northerly winds creates excellent conditions for migration of both passerines and raptors. Many duck species can stand the cold, but when freshwater lakes start to freeze over, they need to move south to find some open water.

Conversely, warm fall and winter weather, as Manhattan experienced in late 2011, can discourage migration among some so-called "half-hardy" species, such as Great Blue Heron, Brown Thrasher, Hermit Thrush, Eastern Phoebe, Orange-crowned Warbler and Gray Catbird.

23

MASTERING MIGRATION

April is when the demands of big year birding rise dramatically. Each day brings the promise of new migrants, and adding two or three new birds in a day is common. Some days will bring six or even more!

I wanted to hold onto my lead, and I was willing to put in the work. My plan had three components:

Research
Before going birding each morning, I needed to have a general idea of what species to expect. eBird was tremendously helpful to this end. I could view a list of all species that have ever appeared in spring migration in Manhattan and a bar-chart plot of their relative frequency of occurrence by week of the month. For example, in early April there is a very high chance of seeing a Yellow-rumped Warbler; there is almost no chance of seeing a Mourning Warbler. Experienced birders have a sense of the general order of migration, but anyone can see it graphically by using eBird's tools.

eBird also began a feature that now has its own website, *Bird-Cast*. This site uses meteorological data and reported sightings to suggest what species will be seen and when the best days are to go birding. If you have to miss birding days, it is best not to miss the potentially great ones. *BirdCast* helps you figure out when those days might be.

I had started taking a quick look at National Weather Service radar for signs of migration before going to bed, even though I planned to bird nearly every day regardless of conditions.

I also had to know what birds were seen the previous day in Manhattan. For this I relied on the online message boards eBirdsNYC and NYSBirds along with reports from eBird. All three would automatically email me with new postings. eBird had a particularly useful feature for a big year birder, the "Your Needs" reports: as soon as anyone reported a species I had not observed in my selected county (New York), I got an email alert with information about the observation.

Birding

Central Park is the best place in Manhattan to see spring migrants, and this is where I would do nearly all of my birding. I would plan on joining Starr Saphir for most of her scheduled morning bird walks. Starr is brilliant at finding unusual birds, and it would also be good to have her respected judgment backing these observations. Having a birding group with many pairs of eyes also helps achieve a high species count. I would also do plenty of birding on my own, sometimes visiting in the afternoon the side of the park that Starr's walk did not cover and going it entirely alone on her days off. Most of my birding would be combined with running to get me to and from birding areas, so I could save time by not having to train later.

Monitoring messages and alerts—crowd-sourcing

Central Park, in particular the Ramble, attracts hundreds of birders during spring migration. Many use their smartphones to post rare bird observations immediately to the message boards. I had my Gmail account set up to relay these posts to me in text-message form. Beginning in mid-April, there were also text alerts from the NYNYBIRD group.

NYNYBIRD is a low-cost system for relaying sightings of rare birds in Manhattan via text-messages. Anders Peltomaa set it up; it is based on similar services that had become popular in Brooklyn and Long Island. It is a powerful innovation with huge benefits for the big year birder.

Prior to it, rare bird postings were infrequent and often too late to be of value. Not all birders had smartphones, and even those who did found it time-consuming to post to the message boards. They would put it off until they finished birding and sat down at their computers. Many of the board postings were of complete birding lists for the day or of extremely rare species. Quick, informal messages about sightings seemed a little out of place.

But nearly everyone has a cell phone capable of sending text messages, which by necessity have to be short. Once you sign up for NYNYBIRD, all you have to do to report a sighting is send a simple text message with the species name and the location. Within seconds, all subscribers have the info.

The new system was perfect for me. I bird in running shoes and running clothes. I can get to another point in the Ramble in less than two minutes. Even if I am at home, I can reach a Ramble alert in ten minutes and a North End alert in fifteen.

24

APRIL ABUNDANCE

When everyone else is focusing on warblers it pays to keep a broader point of view. All species count the same, and you get an advantage only by getting species that other birders miss.

I really wanted the Common Loon (yes, *again*) after it had been observed at the restored saltmarsh on Randall's Island in late March. Twice I ran across the RFK Bridge to the saltmarsh and back, and both times I did not see the Loon. Before I could run again, on April 5, someone noted a Common Loon on the Reservoir in Central Park. This time I found it within minutes.

Snowy Egret, the smaller relative of the Great Egret, is a hard bird to get in Central Park. You can see Great Egrets almost every spring day on water bodies like Turtle Pond and the Meer. Snowy Egrets are more often seen as flyovers, which can make ID more difficult—you have to pick out the dark bill (or yellow feet) against the sky. I was delighted to see a Snowy Egret perched on the dike of the Reservoir at close range on April 17.

Fish Crows look almost the same as regular American Crows, but they make a different sound: a nasal *"awp"* as opposed to a harsh *"caw."* They occur in Central Park but are much less common there than American Crows. I suspect that they are under-reported—you have to be listening for their sound to positively observe them. I heard one flying over the Ramble very early on the Fourth.

Savannah Sparrow is another difficult bird to find in Central Park. Like most sparrows, it is almost always seen foraging on the ground, so if you are just looking for passerines in the trees, you will miss it. It closely resembles the much commoner Song Sparrow, but it has crisper breast streaks and some yellow above the eyes. I had one in the North End on the Sixth and several times thereafter.

Northern Harrier is even harder to get. Your best chance is in fall migration, in mid-October to early November. My only sighting of the entire year was a high flyover on the morning of the Eighth.

Of the three falcons that are regularly seen over Central Park, Merlin is the most difficult to observe. American Kestrel is fairly common and can be seen hunting over areas like the Great Hill and the Great Lawn. Peregrine Falcons nest in Manhattan and often soar over the park, though you may not see one every day. Merlins are also seen mostly in flyovers, but on the 14th I got a special treat: my life Merlin, perched just overhead in a clearing in the North Woods.

On the same day, after I had finished birding the North End and gone home to prepare for lunch with my girlfriend, a report appeared online of a Wilson's Snipe resting at the marshy Upper Lobe in the Ramble. Just prior to this, I had also heard of a Yellow-throated Warbler in Riverside Park. Both are mega-rare birds for Manhattan—what was I to do? I barely had 20 minutes, so I chose the one that was a sure thing and that was closer—the Wilson's Snipe.

In retrospect, I made the right call, as two weeks later another Yellow-throated Warbler appeared, this time in the Ramble, where I was already birding with Starr. We answered the alert and re-found the bird.

On a walk with Starr in the North Woods on the 17th, we were alerted to a rare bird the old-fashioned way, by word of mouth. A longtime birder told Starr that he had seen an American Bittern perching in a tree on the other side of the woods.

The American Bittern, a long-necked, solitary wading bird of marshes, is not recorded in Central Park every year. Its frequency might be more like two or three times per decade. I was very fortunate to respond quickly to an online posting the prior spring and see one hiding along the shore of the Lake in the Ramble. I did not expect to have another the very next year. This one remained in the tree all day and many birders got to see it.

In my rookie year of 2011 I had neglected to look for shorebirds. I was not about to make this mistake again. Central Park regularly gets two shorebirds, Solitary Sandpiper and Spotted Sandpiper, with the latter being a bit more common. They are larger than warblers, smaller than robins, and well-camouflaged for the muddy shoreline areas they prefer. The Lake, the Meer, and the Loch are, in decreasing order, the best places to look for them.

After birding the North End with Starr on the 24th and running back home, I soon got a call from her. She had been told of a Solitary Sandpiper near the Compost Heap, which is just west of the Conservatory Garden. I ran right back out there—I was not about to let tired legs keep me from a life bird. I did not see it, and some fifteen minutes of searching did not turn it up. I suspected it had gone to the nearby Meer, where I soon found it flitting back and forth along the southeast shore.

The next day, on Starr's Ramble walk, I saw a Spotted Sandpiper patrolling the west shore of the Lake by the planted area known as Hernshead. I was relieved to have gotten my two Central Park shorebirds well before most birders had had either one.

There are three gulls that birders can reliably get in large numbers every day of the year in Central Park: Herring Gull, Ring-billed Gull, and Great Black-backed Gull. Just go to the Reservoir, where there are hundreds, sometimes thousands of gulls.

There is a fourth gull that is common on the East River and the Harbor from May through August but that sometimes also appears in small numbers on the Reservoir: Laughing Gull. I believe that few Central Park birders bother to look for them. I saw two of them on the Reservoir on the 25th.

NYNYBIRD alerts were providing rarities, too. On the morning of the 19th, a Great Horned Owl was seen in the Ramble, and after some flying it roosted near the top of a tree adjacent to Evodia Field. Alerts went out quickly, and soon over a hundred people, some birders and many nearby primary-school students, were gathered around gazing almost directly up at it.

I had never seen so much enthusiasm over a bird. While looking for other species later in the day, I was often approached by birders asking if I knew about the owl and offering to direct me to it.

Having already gotten my Great Horned Owl in Inwood Hill Park in February, after much research and effort, I was not exactly thrilled to have this one appear and be observed and listed by everyone.

One of the most remarkable mornings of the spring migration was Saturday, April 21. At 7:15 a.m., as I was heading out the door to bird with Starr in the North End, an alert from Jacob Drucker told of Prothonotary, Worm-eating, and Orange-crowned Warblers at the Wildflower Meadow. I spoke to Starr, who had also heard of the sightings, and we agreed to meet at their location. It took 20 minutes of searching to re-find the Orange-crowned. Then the Prothonotary was seen in the Loch, and behind me at least thirty birders followed as I raced to get to it. The bird was fairly cooperative, and nearly everyone got great views. For me and surely for many others, it was a life bird.

The excitement soon continued. As we were watching the Prothonotary, an alert from just 200 yards up the hill noted a Blue Grosbeak! Jacob, several others, and I took off running again. When we arrived, we heard that the grosbeak had flown across the transverse path to a small hill known as the Grassy Knoll. We followed it, and soon had brief but clear views of the bird.

Shortly thereafter we saw and heard the Worm-eating Warbler, and about an hour after this I answered another alert and added a Cape May Warbler, found initially by Richard Fried. It was singing high in a tree at an entrance to the Great Hill.

All of the above are rarities but in particular the Prothonotary and the Blue Grosbeak, which can take years of Central Park birding to add to one's life list. I began to sense that this would be a special year for Manhattan birding.

Less than a week later, on the 27th, a Kentucky Warbler was found in the area just west of Shakespeare Garden. I ran to it from Turtle Pond, but after a half-hour of waiting the bird did not reappear. Later the same day another alert was issued, and this time the Kentucky showed itself readily.

The Kentucky Warbler is one of the few rarest of those warblers that appear regularly in Central Park.

My auditory skills came through for me on the 29th, when I heard the sharp, distinctive song of the White-eyed Vireo in the Maintenance Meadow and soon saw the bird.

They came through again on the 30th, when I responded to a 7:15 a.m. report of an Orchard Oriole in the Maintenance Meadow. Though I never saw the bird, which appeared to be high in a tree, hidden inside the foliage, I heard its whistled song and this was all I needed.

As for the month of April, I scorched it! I added 46 birds to finish at 131, good for an 18-bird lead on the field. Jacob Drucker had briefly gotten within 6 birds early in the month, but attending college in Massachusetts prevented him from continuing the pace. Andrew Farnsworth appeared to be birding only sporadically, with no reports after the 16th. He was a whopping 28 birds behind. Had he lost interest in the big year lead? He had only two weeks to avoid carrying a large deficit into the fall.

My concern early in the year was that it would be relatively easy to lead when overall birding interest was low but that last year's top birders would pull ahead during migration season, when superior birding skill and experience would be better rewarded. Precisely the opposite was happening—I was increasing *my* lead. I now had a decent shot at finishing in first place, something I would not have thought was possible four months ago.

25

FALLOUT!

When weather forces large masses of migrating birds to land, the term for it is *fallout*. Light rain in the very early morning hours of May 2 likely caused a fallout event over Central Park, and it led to a phenomenal day of birding.

The day began with a bird alert, sent at 7:10 a.m., of Yellow-throated Vireo, Orchard Oriole, and a great variety of warblers at Strawberry Fields, a forested area with great tree diversity on a hill just west of the Lake, near 72nd Street. I had planned to bird with Starr and her group, but upon this news I went directly to Strawberry Fields and called Starr to alert her to the conditions and to encourage her to bring the group there as soon as possible.

Today was far superior to any previous day of the year for birding in two ways: 1) we had far more migrants everywhere you looked; 2) we had an influx of *new* migrants, most notably tanagers, orioles, and some flycatchers. On our best recent days we would have a variety of the more unusual warblers, but we would have just one of each, with over 90% of warblers we observed being Yellow-rumped. Weather conditions (e.g., rain and unfavorable winds) had been discouraging migration, and clearly there was great pent-up demand among migrants to move north.

When I arrived in Strawberry Fields around 7:35 a.m., things were visibly different. Every tree had songbirds dancing from branch to branch. It was going to be a special day.

Many were looking at the Yellow-throated Vireo, about 20 feet high in trees at the south end of Strawberry, and I sighted it quickly. It is one of the three rare vireos (the others are Philadelphia and White-eyed) in Central Park, historically observed a little less often than a Worm-eating Warbler—which is to say, a very rare bird that for some will be a life bird.

High atop a nearby tree was a juvenile Orchard Oriole, much less common than the Baltimore Oriole, and also a first-of-year bird for me.

In the trees to the south someone noticed a spot of brilliant red: the year's first male Scarlet Tanager.

When Starr's group arrived, we had a problem: as soon as someone pointed out a good bird, like a Blue-headed Vireo (of which there were many today), someone else would pipe in with another one, like a Blue-winged Warbler (another we heard and saw often). The frenetic pace continued throughout the morning.

Gray skies and frequent showers made for difficult viewing conditions, but birds were abundant enough that eventually we had good looks at all species. Starr pointed out that the overcast, cool conditions actually helped us continue to get warblers with very little drop off as the morning wore on, which would not have been the case on a sunny, hot day.

Starr re-found the Yellow-throated Vireo. We saw Red-eyed Vireos, too, and later, at Hernshead, a Warbling Vireo—a bird that we often hear, but rarely see. Starr spotted her first-of-season Ruby-throated Hummingbird at Strawberry Fields; I had mine in the Maintenance Meadow.

My new warblers for the year were Canada, Black-throated Blue, Magnolia, and American Redstart.

We heard Rose-breasted Grosbeak (new for the year)

throughout much of the Ramble, though we never saw it. Still, it counts.

While we were at Turtle Pond we received a text alert of a Kentucky Warbler at Azalea Pond, so we set off toward it. By the time we arrived, perhaps twelve minutes later, the bird was no longer being seen. The text alerts do not always work out. I would respond to many over the course of spring migration and, in a small minority of cases, would fail to get the bird.

The alerts worked very well for most warblers, which tend to remain on or near a tree that is providing them with food. They worked much less well for flycatchers, as you will see later. Flycatchers often dart away quickly and disappear from view.

Our consolation prize for missing the Kentucky was a handsome Wood Thrush we saw along the way. It was not a new bird for the season, but I was glad to see it nonetheless. It is easy to get so caught up in the big year quest that the joy of birding is lost. I was still having a lot of fun. Then again, it was early May. How would I feel in November?

Today was providing both great beauty and impressive numbers. The area just north of Azalea had a trove of good birds including more Scarlet Tanagers.

Elsewhere in the Ramble, Starr had her first Veery of the year, but this skulking bird shied away before I could see it. The Veery had already been on my mind, as others were reporting it regularly in the Ramble for several days, but I was not finding any, and this bothered me. How could I miss a reasonably large, ground-dwelling bird that lots of birders were seeing? I searched for it specifically the next day and still did not get it. I should have just accepted that it is a fairly common bird and that eventually I would see it. Big years encourage—and also reward—obsession, which I would have to try to keep in check.

After five hours into the walk, we responded to a text alert of a Cape May Warbler near the Rustic Shelter. Starr and I heard it upon arriving (its high *seet-seet-seet-seet* song stands out against lower-pitched chatter) but we did not see it. We did, however, get to both hear and see a Blackburnian Warbler.

Later, I saw a perching thrush fly off. I was hoping it would be a Veery, but Starr re-found it farther away and it turned out to be a Swainson's Thrush, also a new bird for the year.

After nearly six hours of birding, a rough estimate had us around 68 birds for the day. Starr wanted us to have 70—she always went for the round number, and to willingly fall short would be an admission of defeat. Hearing a Song Sparrow got us one bird closer. By then the rain had started coming down more heavily and, with the temperature around 50, I was chilled.

Starr was not dressed any more warmly, but she actually considered birding Strawberry Fields again on the way out of the park! We quickly realized this was not a good idea, and decided to call it a day. Starr and Lenore performed a careful recount under subway shelter and found that we had indeed reached our target of 70.

Starr's unflagging enthusiasm and energy made this a memorable day. I include it in detail not only because it shows what birding is like under fallout conditions, but also because it shows Starr at her best. Her walks were an essential part of my big year. Without them I would have observed less and learned less.

Starr had elected to take an extended break from chemotherapy so that she could lead her walks during the spring and enjoy birding the way she always had—passionately. She was literally risking her life in order to bird with us.

Here was a 72-year-old woman beset by a host of physical infirmities—a bad back, a pronounced limp, and painful arthritis—along with metastatic cancer, brilliantly leading us for six hours in the cold rain across the hills of Central Park, seeing and hearing everything, patiently and deftly guiding all members of the group with her words alone (never pointing) and wanting to go on longer still, simply so that we could observe more birds. Starr always knew how to inspire.

26

THE REST OF MAY

The day after Starr's big walk, Thursday, May 3, I was out in the Ramble on my own until I ran into Joe DiCostanzo's American Museum of Natural History Group. Stephen Quinn was in the process of retiring from giving walks, and DiCostanzo was both doing his own walks and covering Quinn's.

I helped find the group some good birds including another Yellow-throated Vireo just outside the Belvedere Castle plaza. It was a relaxing, easygoing walk in which I also added two new warblers for the year, both of which Starr had yesterday but that I had not observed: Blackpoll Warbler and Chestnut-sided Warbler. The former is particularly easy to get because its high-pitched *tsit-tsit-tsit-tsit-tsit-tsit* call sounds almost mechanical and unlike anything else. The latter is less common and much more colorful. DiCostanzo spotted it on the path from Tupelo Meadow to Belvedere Castle.

After I finished birding, my lunch was interrupted by an online posting regarding an interesting sparrow seen in Central Park. One expert birder thought it might be a Grasshopper Sparrow, an extremely rare bird for the park and one not seen every year; another birder was less sure.

I knew that I needed to see this bird just in case it turned out to be the Grasshopper or perhaps some other member of the rare *Ammodramus* genus. The location of the bird was clear—it was hanging around one of the fenced-in lawn bowling fields north of Sheep Meadow. Somehow, though, I misinterpreted the location and ended up searching near the Great Lawn, over a half-mile away. I still cannot see how I made this mistake! Needless to say, I did not see the bird.

I was OK with not seeing it, however, because it seemed very questionable, with an unconvincing photo. That is, until a second posting about it appeared. Soon after this posting the bird's finder along with one of my close big year competitors, Anders Peltomaa, both entered their sightings into eBird and officially claimed to have observed a Grasshopper Sparrow.

I had made a huge mistake! I considered searching the lawn bowling area at first light the next day to see if the Grasshopper Sparrow had lingered. When an early morning alert told of a Yellow-billed Cuckoo on the Great Hill, I decided to run for this nemesis bird first. The location given was vague, however, and when I arrived I found neither the reporter nor the cuckoo.

Then my luck changed. Other birders had gone to look for the Grasshopper, and at 8:20 a.m. I received a text alert that it had been re-found near its prior location in the Falconer's Hill area.

I ran directly to the West 103rd Street stop on the C line and took the train to 72nd Street. From there I ran to Falconer's Hill, where I saw several birders watching the Grasshopper Sparrow. I got a good view of it perching low in a tree atop the hill by the rocks. Now I had the bird, and yesterday's mistake no longer mattered. It was species 145 of the year.

As I was walking back through the Ramble, another alert arrived, this one of a Cerulean Warbler at the Captain's Bench. I needed a Cerulean Warbler, one of the few rarest of the regularly-occurring warbler species in Central Park. The problem was that, though I had memorized all the common park location nicknames seen on birding maps, I did not know where to find the Captain's Bench. So I just kept on walking home, figuring that I would look it up online.

I was amazed that even the internet could not tell me clearly where the Captain's Bench was! A posting later that day finally had the answer: it was the bench at the top of a sloping meadow just north of the Point and northeast of the Loeb Boathouse entrance to the Ramble. It is a great place to see birds.

Before I learned this, though, another bird alert made the information unnecessary: the Cerulean had been re-found near Willow Rock. I was on the run again. Roughly twenty birders were circling the area, and soon someone spotted the bird on a nearby branch, and I got a brief but clear view.

As I was walking back through Maintenance Meadow, I saw a something larger than a sparrow moving in the brush. I waited for the bird to turn so I could get a full view, and when it did a wave of relief came over me: it was the Veery! Now my birding day was complete. I had gotten one the toughest birds and one of the easiest birds, but they both counted the same.

My Saturday walk in the North End with Starr the next day, May 5, added another four species including Bay-breasted Warbler, a bird rare enough to merit an alert, and Indigo Bunting, more common but still one of the most sought-after birds of spring migration, as the males appear vibrantly blue all over. Starr pointed out that the Indigo Bunting, like all other North American birds with blue feathers, does not actually produce blue pigment. It has tiny structures on its feathers that refract light and cause them to appear blue.

These four species got me to 151 for the year, which was one more than my total for all of 2011. I was on a torrid pace, but suddenly my lead was shrinking. Andrew Farnsworth got back to birding with some masterful outings of 60 or more species. His total for the year was now 141. Clearly, he had not given up!

Anders Peltomaa, now only 16 back at 135, was gaining on me. The always-dangerous Jacob Drucker was birding Manhattan again, and he was at 125. This was no time to coast!

Ever since Starr got her Lincoln's Sparrow on the Second, I was wondering when I would get mine. Lincoln's is tough for a few reasons: first, there are just not very many of them and they tend to be lone birds; second, they are shy skulkers, not staying in open view for long, which means that alerts are less effective; third, most birders are not trying to find them, so they do not get reported as much as they probably should. Still, several other birders had had a Lincoln's within the last couple days and I was annoyed that I was not among them.

I answered an alert for one on the morning of Sunday the Sixth, but I got to it quite late and the exact location, where it had also been reported the day before, was not given precisely. I strolled over to nearby Falconer's Hill and had what would be my last look at the Grasshopper Sparrow. I also had my first White-crowned Sparrow of the year in Central Park (a bird I had already had for the year in Union Square over the winter).

I vowed to be ready to bird early on Monday the Seventh, but I was not early enough—the alert on the Lincoln's arrived close to 6 a.m., when I was still in bed. I hurriedly downed my breakfast and put on my running clothes, setting off for a more exact location this time, one near the Naumburg Bandshell. As I approached I saw two birders standing near where I expected to see the bird. I ran on the side of plantings opposite them, a decision that paid off: the Lincoln's Sparrow appeared ten feet ahead of me. I stopped to admire it briefly, and then got out of there.

It was 6:45 a.m. I had 45 minutes before Starr's Ramble walk. I wanted to look around the Point on my own, as it can be a good spot for warblers and flycatchers. I did not have long to relax. At 7:10 an alert arrived of the season's first Summer Tanager; it was seen and heard near Tanner's Spring.

Summer Tanager is recorded mostly during spring migration in Central Park, where it is very rare—about as rare as White-eyed Vireo, for example.

I did not want to miss it, so I started running fast, out the Ramble over Bank Rock Bridge and then north on the park's West Drive. As I was running I saw Anders Peltomaa walking on same the side of the road, going in the opposite direction. I assumed he was coming back from having seen the Summer Tanager. After all, he had set up the bird alert system, and there was no other way I could explain him walking away from where a nearby rarity awaited. He said something to me as we were about to pass, but I could not make it out, and I did not want to stop. I had my rhythm going and was close to getting a great bird, so I just waved at him—to put it charitably. I suspect it came across more as "Talk to the hand—I am in a hurry!"

I expected to see other birders at Tanner's Spring—at the very least, the ones who issued the alert. I had arrived in well under ten minutes, so they could not have gone far. I checked the trees across the drive. There was no sign of the bird or of the birders. I ran up to Summit Rock and still saw no one. This was strange.

By then it must have been close to 7:30, and I needed to call Starr—who does not get the text-message alerts and whose group was meeting only a couple blocks away—and encourage her to bring the group to the Summit Rock area first. Everyone would want to try for the Summer Tanager.

Meanwhile, *I* still needed to find it. I ran back down to Tanner's Spring and finally saw a group of birders standing on the upslope with Anthony Collerton. By now I was faintly hearing Summer Tanager song.

As I approached the birders, I saw someone I did not expect to see: Anders Peltomaa. This was going to be awkward!

I explained to them that I was looking for the Summer Tanager, and they got me on it visually right away. Before I could try to discuss what just happened, Starr and the group arrived. The focus switched to getting her and the others on the bird, which had just flown to a closer tree. One of the birders already present used his arm to point at the bird (rather than giving a verbal description of the bird's location), and the bird immediately flew again. Starr's critique came quickly and sharply: "I tell people do NOT point at birds because 80% of the time it makes them fly, and this is exactly what happened."

The Summer Tanager did not fly far, however, and soon everyone was back on it. I joined Starr, and we went on our way as the other birders wandered off. One potential disaster (the group missing the Summer Tanager) had been averted, but I still had a problem of my own with which to deal.

I emailed Anders after I got back from the walk, explaining that I assumed he was returning from having seen the Summer Tanager when I encountered him. He wrote that he had forgotten to take his cell phone with him that morning and so he had not gotten the bird alert. But, he went on, he knew that only the report of a very good bird would make me run so fast and single-mindedly, so he had the good sense to turn around and walk after me. He just happened to better time his arrival with the reappearance of Collerton and friends. He graciously accepted my apology.

I was treating the eBird "Top Birders" list as a serious competition, and I was playing to win. Nonetheless, birding with others in a public park demands coöperation and civility. We all rely on each other's postings and alerts, and we encounter each other often while birding. I needed to remind myself not to be a jerk.

I was having a great spring migration season, observing nearly all the expected warblers, tanagers, and vireos. The problem is that a couple of other birders, including Peltomaa, were doing just as well. My lead consisted largely of birds I had gotten in the winter; as far as spring migrants were concerned, these men had caught up and were now matching me bird-for-bird. With flycatchers, cuckoos, and some other unusual birds still to come, I could not afford any misses.

I was already thinking about cuckoos. They are just a bit larger than Blue Jays, and vary in abundance from year to year. They can be easier to get in the fall, as they were in 2011 when Yellow-billed Cuckoo was seen frequently in Maintenance Meadow. There had already been a few reports of this species in recent days, including the previously-mentioned one on the Great Hill. I still had not observed it.

There are two species, Yellow-billed and Black-billed, and they differ mainly as their names suggest. The latter is less common. They have distinctive sounds and can be loud, but when passing through Central Park they tend to be quiet. They are hard to observe because they often sit motionless and alone on branches of deciduous trees waiting to pick off caterpillars.

On the morning of Friday, May 11, I was already running toward the North End when I received a text alert of a Black-billed Cuckoo at the Captain's Bench. This time I knew exactly where to go, so I turned around and ran the mile back toward the Ramble. I even managed to encounter the two birders who issued the alert, still nearby. They told me where they saw the bird. I went there, aside the actual bench, but did not see it. I soon heard its *"coo-coo-coo-coo"* call, though, and this was sufficient.

Black-billed Cuckoo turned out to be the only species on my 2012 list that I never observed visually. I would hear it again in October with Lenore Swenson, then even more clearly.

As for Yellow-billed, that would go on to be one of my few major misses of the spring season, even as it was observed by nearly every other top birder.

The Gray-cheeked Thrush is one of drabbest birds of spring migration, and finding it is no fun. I wait until it starts being reported, and then I begin the painstaking task of examining all similar thrushes closely, looking for one whose eye-ring is pale and incomplete and whose face and top side are gray-brown. It is often a judgment call—a tricky one in poor light. I saw mine in the North End with Starr on the 12th.

Flycatchers are much more exciting to observe. They fly acrobatically and produce plenty of sound. Eastern Phoebe is an abundant early migrant with distinctive looks. Eastern Wood-Pewee arrives later, and though it could potentially be mistaken for other flycatchers based only on appearance, its *"pee-wee"* song leaves no doubt as to identity. Eastern Kingbird and Great Crested Flycatcher are much larger than other flycatchers and are easy to identify visually, though the latter can be a bit harder to find; it helps to listen for its rising *"wee-eep"* call. None of the above birds should elude a regular Central Park birder.

The more difficult flycatchers are the so-called *Empidonax*, more colloquially referred to as empids, and the Olive-sided Flycatcher. The empids occurring in Central Park are Least, Yellow-bellied, Acadian, Willow, and Alder Flycatcher. This list also goes from most to least common. All have distinctive songs by which they can be identified, and this is my preferred ID method for all but the Yellow-bellied. The last two can be conclusively distinguished in the field *only* by their songs.

The Olive-sided Flycatcher can be identified visually. It is larger than the empids, with a dark head and dark flanks, and is less common than the Acadian.

I had already had Least Flycatcher on May 5 and several times thereafter.

On May 14 the Ramble was alive with the forceful *"peet-SAH"* songs of Acadian Flycatchers. On the way to meeting up with Starr I had gotten several alerts of Acadian Flycatchers stretching all the way from aside the Metropolitan Museum to the area just south of Maintenance Meadow. I also got good looks at their handsome green plumage.

On May 16 Starr had a Yellow-bellied Flycatcher in a tree just outside the Belvedere Castle plaza. I caught just a fleeting glimpse of it, but others saw it better and there was no question of identity. I counted it, but I hoped for a better look at one.

The next day I was roused early again by an alert of both Yellow-bellied Flycatcher and Mourning Warbler at Strawberry Fields. Foregoing breakfast, I ran right over. Already fifteen birders were searching the area, including the legendary Al Levantin, one of a trio who in 1998 closely pursued the North American big year record and ended up becoming a featured subject of Mark Obmascik's book *The Big Year*. In the 2011 movie adaptation, the character very loosely based on Levantin was played by Steve Martin. This time neither Levantin nor anyone else who responded to the alert re-found the Mourning Warbler. The Yellow-bellied Flycatcher was seen again over an hour later, by which time I had already left to bird the Ramble.

The following week brought many rainy days and no new birds for me. On May 23, early rain ending by 7 a.m. may have again created fallout conditions. Starr's group ended up having 64 species and 19 warblers, the best-ever day Starr could recall for this late in the season. A single tree at Summit Rock produced 13 warbler species at the beginning of the walk.

The only regularly-occurring spring warbler that I had not gotten was Mourning Warbler. None of the other top birders had it, either. As our group was passing Shakespeare Garden a text alert arrived: Alice Deutsch was reporting a Mourning Warbler singing near 101st Street and Central Park West, roughly a mile away. I figured I could reach it in seven minutes, and off I went.

Once there I saw Alice, who directed me to the bird. Right away I heard it singing *"chirry-chirry-chirry,"* and soon I also saw its distinctive dark face and black breast.

I was thrilled to have gotten a life bird and one of the rarer warblers of Central Park. I had also achieved a perfect spring warbler season, observing all those warblers that regularly occur.

I ran back to the Ramble and re-joined the group at Hernshead. What had Starr been doing in the 25 minutes I was gone? Just getting a Mourning Warbler of her own! She briefly saw a quiet one at the Upper Lobe along with a Bay-breasted Warbler. We would return to the Upper Lobe on the way back to the Ramble and this time all would hear the Mourning Warbler's song, and some would get to see it.

My last Central Park bird of the spring came five days later on May 28. As we were walking east on the path descending from Belvedere Castle, we saw some birds in trees near the shore of Turtle Pond. Some were House Finches, a common species throughout the winter and spring. Starr noticed that one looked a bit different, and it turned out to be a Purple Finch, a species that had been unusually rare in the past six months. I was glad to pick up a bird on nearly the entire field. Had I known then that the fall would bring an epic finch irruption I would have felt much less secure in the value of our find.

Flycatchers were still on my mind. Many birders had gotten an Olive-sided Flycatcher in the Ramble on Saturday, May 5, when I was in the North End with Starr. On May 17 I ran out to the Azalea Pond area three times in response to alerts of Olive-sided Flycatchers. I spent an hour walking back and forth along the Gill after the third alert, expecting the flycatcher would eventually show itself. Soon after I left, Anthony Collerton, whom I had encountered while searching, saw it. This was the same day I had run out early to chase the Yellow-bellied Flycatcher in Strawberry Fields. I was fatigued and clearly much less lucky with flycatchers than I had been with warblers.

I wrote earlier of how I did not want to let the demands of my big year detract too much from the joy of birding. On this day the joy was gone! It was hot, and I had no reason to be out there other than to see a single bird, which somehow managed to hide every time I ran out to look at it. I thought back to the day in January when a ten-mile trek produced only a resident Peregrine that I could have seen any day. I did not get discouraged then, and I was not about to now.

I had hoped that the last two walks of the spring, on May 29 and May 30, could produce another flycatcher, and I did everything I could to put the odds in my favor. I even told Starr what I needed so that her sensitive ears would be listening for the relevant calls and songs. Still, we neither heard nor saw any new flycatchers. I did a few walks on my own in early June with the same results.

By missing the Olive-sided I had lost a bird to the field, but I would still have a chance in the fall to get it and redeem myself.

This was not the case for the Willow Flycatcher; my time to get it had almost certainly passed. The reason was that flycatchers in the fall do not sing, though they may rarely vocalize parts of a song. Without at least some song (or call) it would be impossible to distinguish a Willow Flycatcher from an Alder Flycatcher. The Willow cost me a bird, not to the field but to my two closest competitors.

On May 27 I took the ferry across New York Harbor to Governor's Island. I had learned of a large roosting colony of Common Terns, which are not seen in Central Park. They were easy to find, and they gave me a species that many Manhattan birders would not bother to get (even though they could also be gotten, with patience, from Battery Park). I had hoped also to see the much rarer Forster's Tern, but none appeared.

Governor's Island is an important location for Manhattan birders to know. It is indeed part of Manhattan (like Randall's Island), and it is far enough out in the harbor that it has some birds that might not be seen so easily from the southern tip of the island. It can be a place to see a Laughing Gull, a Forster's Tern, a Black Skimmer, or a Killdeer, among others. It is a great place to hear a Fish Crow.

I finished May, still in first place, with 164 species. Andrew Farnsworth was second with 152, and Anders Peltomaa was third with 148. Jacob Drucker was in fifth with 138. I liked my chances, but the race was far from over. The fall and early winter would offer everyone a second chance to get the birds they had missed. None of the top birders could be counted out, and it was possible that someone even lower on the list would put on a surge and start contending. My biggest concern, though, was meteorological: a summer hurricane could allow Farnsworth, an experienced hurricane birder who could view the East River from the safety of his apartment, to erase nearly his entire deficit in one day.

I had been going at it nearly every day, sometimes all day, since April, and I was looking forward to taking a break from birding. June would be a good time to do so—no new migrants would be on the way until shorebirds start showing up in July.

27

EARLY SUMMER

The migrants clear out of Central Park much more abruptly than they arrive. May 23 had the second-best walk of the spring in terms of both total species and total warbler species. Less than ten days later, with the arrival of June, the migrants had almost entirely left Central Park. The Ramble suddenly grew quiet—the warbler songs that had filled the air were no longer being heard. Maybe you could hear a single Blackpoll Warbler or see a Common Yellowthroat or Great Crested Flycatcher, but you would have a difficult time totaling even 30 species for the day. Why even bother? We had had an unusually good spring—the Appendix offers a detailed analysis—and anyone who tried already had all the warblers he or she could have wanted.

I still needed my Willow and Alder Flycatchers, which can be late arrivals, so I took a few half-hearted walks through the Ramble in early June to try to hear them. The Ramble had become a birding wasteland: hot, humid, fully-foliaged, and free of the desirable birds.

I soon put my birding to rest, and did not record any eBird lists in June.

Andrew Farnsworth eventually roused me back into action. He

chipped away at my lead with some great sightings. On June 18 he observed a Yellow-crowned Night-Heron flying over Roosevelt Island. Then he had Bank Swallow on the 27th, Black Skimmer on the 28th, Killdeer on July 1 (which he had already observed in May), and two birds on July 5: Forster's Tern and Purple Martin. This was six unanswered birds, all seen from the Sutton Place area where he lived. I had to return to action and try for these birds!

My first targets were Forster's Tern and Black Skimmer. Both were found in New York Harbor by the New Jersey piers and off of Brooklyn. The Staten Island Ferry seemed like the logical choice. I rode it at noon on July 8 and saw Common Terns but no Forster's and no Black Skimmer.

I really wanted to see the Black Skimmer because of its distinctive look: it has a very long red and black bill, with the lower mandible even longer than the upper. It is named for its feeding method, which involves flying low over the water with its bill open and letting its lower mandible skim the surface. When it touches a small fish or crustacean, it shuts its bill, trapping its prey.

I was not going to give up easily. That afternoon I ran to the Peter Detmold Park area in Sutton Place at 4 p.m., the same time of day that Farnsworth had had his Forster's Tern and Purple Martin. I even went a few blocks south to view U Thant Island, which was attracting a great many seabirds, including Laughing Gull and Common Tern—but none of the ones I wanted.

A week later I returned to Governor's Island and sorted through hundreds of Common Terns, but I still found no Forster's Terns and did not see any Black Skimmers.

In retrospect, I had made two mistakes: starting too late in the season and going out too late in the day. There had been Forster's Tern sightings from the Staten Island Ferry in mid-June when the birds were still taking their measure of the area. By now, I suspect that most of the species was nesting on the southern coast of New York City and Long Island, with the Jamaica Bay Wildlife Refuge appearing to be a preferred spot. New York Harbor, with its heavily-industrialized waterfront and frequent shipping traffic, was not as desirable a location. As for the Black Skimmer, it was being observed off some New Jersey piers at 7 a.m. It probably did not want to be feeding under the midday sun any more than I wanted to be out there looking for it; it is most active near dawn and dusk, a behavioral fact that I had neglected to learn. I recall taking one more Staten Island Ferry ride and then throwing in the towel on these birds.

My second target was the Yellow-crowned Night-Heron. I searched eBird and noticed that one had been observed on Randall's Island in late June of the previous year. I also saw that the promotional site for Randall's Island displayed a photo of this bird and mentioned that it is known to frequent the island. When I further learned that the 103rd Street footbridge to Randall's Island had just reopened on July 1, I realized that birding there had suddenly become very convenient. I had to go!

From my apartment on the Upper East Side I could run to the footbridge, cross over the East River, and be at the restored salt-marsh by Icahn Stadium in 22 minutes.

The first few times I went, I got nothing new. Then on July 10 I had an Osprey flying over the river. I was surprised that I had not already seen one in the spring, but very few people had. It would be a very easy bird to get in fall migration, but I was still glad to add my first new bird in over a month and reach 165.

On July 13 I decided to take a new approach to Randall's Island on my late-morning run: I took the subway to 125th Street and then entered off the RFK Bridge pedestrian walkway. I figured that the nearby Bronx Kill, a narrow inlet separating Randall's Island from the Bronx to the north, might be a productive spot to try, owing to its proximity to South Brother Island, a well-known nesting site for large colonies of egrets and herons.

After walking across the intervening baseball fields to reach the Bronx Kill, I heard some unusual, high calls, which led me to seeing my first several Killdeers of the year. They were foraging on the shore of the inlet. After my many failed attempts to see this species in January at Swindler Cove, it was a huge relief to finally add it to my list at number 166.

My day was not over yet. After proceeding east across the northern border of the island, I came across another saltmarsh. Posing on the shoreline rocks next to it was a beautiful Yellow-crowned Night-Heron!

Among the leading birders, only Farnsworth had this species, and now I had it, too. I was amazed to see yet another one at the restored saltmarsh further south. What a day!

I had added three new birds in the past four days, reaching 167 and extending the lead I had over Farnsworth to eight birds. Given how easy it was to find the two Yellow-crowneds, and given how rare the species was in Central Park, I figured other top birders would want to visit Randall's Island and also observe these herons. But even though the birds stuck around over the following days, no other birders reported them on eBird, allowing me to gain another bird on the field.

As much as I wanted to also add Purple Martin and Bank Swallow, I saw no reliable way to get them. The former had only a small number of reports in the entire New York City/Long Island area. The species appeared to range mostly to the south and west of New York. The latter had just a few more reports and probably could have been glimpsed flying over the Reservoir at some point during migration. Would I have wanted to devote several hours then to a low-percentage chance to see a single species? Probably not, and the odds off seeing it were even lower in mid-July. I chose not to pursue these birds now; perhaps I would come across them during fall migration.

There was one species that it would not take any luck to get, and Farnsworth did not have it: Monk Parakeet. I recalled from 2011 that the area in West Harlem near 140th Street and the Hudson Greenway was a great spot to see these colorful, noisy birds. I went there on July 22 and before I even got to the Greenway I heard the unmistakable, squawking call of the Monk Parakeet on 138th Street near Riverside Drive. It became bird number 168.

28

SHOREBIRD EXPLOSION

At 10 a.m. on July 30, Jacob Drucker reported online that he just had 15 Semipalmated Sandpipers at Swindler Cove Park. Shorebird season was on! I figured the afternoon would be even better, as the tide would be near its low, and I went up there right after lunch.

I saw at least 40 Semipalmated Sandpipers, the highest total reported in recent years at Swindler. It was a very promising start to the season.

I also saw what I am *almost* certain was a Short-billed Dowitcher. It had a red-tinged, buffy breast and a very long bill. It exhibited the "sewing machine" feeding behavior that typifies the species. It was also taller and much larger than the nearby Semipalmated Sandpipers. But, with just my binoculars, I could not get a great view. It certainly was *something* new, but what? I was by no means a shorebird expert. It could have been a Long-billed Dowitcher with a bit less rufous than most.

Initially I entered it as a Short-billed Dowitcher, but it bothered me that this species had never before been reported on eBird at Swindler Cove. I believe that the standards have be to very high when you are reporting a new species. I wrote to Andrew Farnsworth, who is responsible for approving eBird observations of rare species in Manhattan, and he suggested that if I was not totally sure, I should list it as *Large Shorebird Sp.*, which would not add to my species total, and then put in the comments my reasons for suspecting Short-billed Dowitcher. So this is what I did, and I felt that it was the right thing to do. I also believed that I would have many chances to see the bird again.

I returned the following afternoon and did not see anything new, nor did I see the possible dowitcher.

Late in the evening on Friday, August 3, an eBird report said that Jacob Drucker had gotten two Least Sandpipers and a Semipalmated Plover at Swinder Cove. I called Starr Saphir the following day and suggested that she join me for birding Swindler at low tide around 4 p.m. on Sunday. Starr had not had any of the new shorebirds from Swindler yet this year and she was excited to go.

She arrived on Sunday just after I did, around 3:45. At our first observation point well above the mudflats, we saw an enormous flock of Semipalmated Sandpipers, easily 150, many times more than had ever been recorded there before. Starr also picked out some Least Sandpipers, which I was having a harder time finding.

We decided to move to a superior vantage point directly adjacent to the flats, in back of the compost heap, where the best sightings on Friday had occurred. Several Semipalmated Plovers (which look like Killdeer but are smaller and have only one dark neck ring) immediately came into view. With them were the Least Sandpipers, darker brown and with droopier bills than the Semipalmated. Mission accomplished! I had 171 total species, seven ahead of Farnsworth.

We took a walk further inside the park just to see whatever might be around. My concern quickly shifted from the birds to Starr. She had already started feeling very tired just 20 minutes into our birding while we were watching the Least Sandpipers. I found this a bit unsettling. We had not needed to walk more than two hundred yards, and Starr had even taken some time to sit on an observation bench. She had arrived in a cab, so she had done little walking beforehand. Granted, the weather was hot (90 degrees) and humid (dew point 72) but not unusually so for August in New York, and we mostly were in the shade.

Starr had managed a two-hour walk in the hilly North End on May 29 under similar conditions. The difference was that she was not on chemotherapy then. At least I *hoped* that was the only difference. Starr's walks would be starting again in two weeks and there was no way she could give one in her current condition.

I suggested that she might not be getting enough nutrition to keep her energy level up, and I gave her a Zone bar, which I carry with me for energy in the field. She pointed out that cancer feeds off of sugars (a fact that had just begun to reach the population at large) and that she had adopted a very low-glycemic-index diet years ago on her doctor's advice in order to help suppress the cancer. I believe this was a brilliant move on her part and one that required immense discipline. She had been beating metastatic breast cancer for an amazing ten years. Perhaps this was one of her secrets?

I had also lowered my sugar intake some years ago for precisely this reason—the link with cancer. I knew that muscles recovered better after strenuous exercise when *some* simple sugars were consumed, and I did a lot of strenuous exercise. But, other than a post-workout energy bar, I had eliminated foods with additional sugars and I felt better for having done so.

Getting back to shorebirds, an online report said that a Lesser Yellowlegs had been seen at the Inwood Hill Park mud flats (which are a 15-minute walk from Swindler Cove) on Sunday the Fifth. So on Tuesday I returned to visit both locations, and though I once again saw the shorebirds I had seen with Starr, I did not find the Lesser Yellowlegs or any other large shorebirds.

This leads to another remarkable Starr Saphir story. I was doing some reading online on Friday, August 11, around 9:35 p.m. when Starr telephoned me. She had just had a Lesser Yellowlegs on the Inwood Hill flats. I asked her how this was possible; it had been dark for well over an hour. She explained that her daughter Shawna, who lives with her near Inwood Hill, had been walking along the shore in the twilight and had seen an unusual bird. So Shawna told Starr, who then went out to look for the bird. The streetlights provided just enough illumination, and she saw the Lesser Yellowlegs right where Shawna had said it was.

I quickly debated whether or not to take a 45-minute trip uptown to look for a shorebird in the dark. I would not have time to try for it tomorrow—Saturday was girlfriend day—and besides, it could fly at dawn and be gone. It would, however, almost certainly still be around if I looked tonight. Putting it that way made the decision easy!

I was out the door by 10 p.m., but a long wait for the C train followed by a long wait for the A train meant that I did not enter Inwood Hill Park until 11 p.m.

I did not like what I saw when I arrived. Unlike Central Park at night, Inwood Hill did not have runners or people enjoying a quiet cross-town stroll. It appeared empty and mostly unlit, but I did not have to go through any woods, just open, grassy areas and baseball fields, so I broke into an easy run and headed for the shore of the salt-marsh at the bottom of the hill.

The shore had some street lights ringing it, but they were much fewer and less bright than I had hoped. It was just an hour after low tide. At first glance I saw nothing but darkness. How had Starr seen this shorebird? Then I tried my binoculars, searching areas near the street lights. I soon saw the outline of a large bird, but too large, and with much too thick a bill—a Black-

Crowned Night-Heron, living up to its name by feeding at night. The flashlight I had brought along did little good. I saw some other birds further out, but after a half-hour of searching I could not re-find the Lesser Yellowlegs; I figured it had found a great hiding spot and was at rest.

There was also another issue: I had wanted to use the men's room before I even entered the park, and I *really* wanted to use it now, despite not taking in any fluids on the way. The restrooms by the tennis courts almost surely would be locked at this hour, not that I would try using them in a dark, deserted park. Public restrooms can be maddeningly hard to find on the streets of Manhattan, but they are plentiful in the city's parks. Tonight they would do me no good. With an uncomfortable hour's commute awaiting me, it was time to get out.

This was not my only night birding effort of the year. Back on January 17, I had gone out to the Central Park Pinetum area at 7:45 p.m. to listen for a Barred Owl that Jacob Drucker had reported at 5:15. I never heard it.

I figured that the good shorebirding would continue, as the season usually runs well into September, but the large flocks of Semipalmated Sandpipers soon grew smaller. I made one more afternoon visit to Swindler Cove on August 17 and saw nothing new. A Lesser Yellowlegs was photographed there a week later (by someone who observed the mudflats for five straight hours), but by then the regular fall migrants were moving and I was back to birding Central Park and tired of the long commute to Swindler Cove.

I had a decent summer and an excellent shorebird season, observing all the species that had appeared in decent numbers, and gaining at least a couple more birds than everyone except for Farnsworth, who amazingly got the same shorebirds from his perch in Sutton Place looking out toward Roosevelt Island.

As of August 17, I had 171 birds, with Farnsworth at 164 and

Peltomaa further back at 153. No one else was in the running anymore, though I still wondered if Jacob Drucker at 142, hampered by having to be away at college, would put on a late-year surge, as he did last year, and give everyone a scare. He had gotten the shorebirds, and the fall would give him another shot at the migrants he missed in the spring. Had he been able to bird Manhattan every day, he certainly would have been contending for the big year lead.

I had been maintaining a spreadsheet listing the species I had not yet seen and my best guess as to the probability of seeing them. For example, the Sharp-shinned Hawk seemed almost a lock for the fall, so I assigned it 0.95 (95%). The Bald Eagle was less likely, but still even-odds, so I gave it 0.5. The Connecticut Warbler seemed like a total long shot, so I gave it only 0.1. When I added up all these probabilities, I got to 190, my expected finishing total. In a normal year, this is probably where I would have ended up. The fall of 2012, however, would prove to be anything but normal.

29

FINCH IRRUPTION

Starr Saphir's fall birding season began with a private walk given to some parents and their youngsters on Sunday, August 19. As soon as it ended, around 11 a.m., she called me from her cell to let me know that she had observed an Alder Flycatcher calling at Hernshead, by the Lake, at 9 a.m.

I needed to make up for my poor spring flycatcher performance, but I held out little hope of re-finding Starr's Alder. Normally, Starr would call me immediately from her regular walks if she found a great bird and I was away; she wisely did not want to risk offending her new clients, who did not know me, and so her news came much too late to help me. I ran to Hernshead for a cursory search, but that flycatcher could have been at the other end of the park by now. Still, knowing that one had been around gave me hope that others might appear.

A bird of particular interest to me was the Red-breasted Nuthatch. It had not been observed in the park during the previous fall, winter, and spring seasons, so I had never had one. Oddly enough, one was reported in the Central Park Ramble in June. There had also been recent reports of them around Greenwich, Connecticut, and just yesterday one was reported by Turtle Pond in the Ramble.

The Red-breasted Nuthatch breeds in the coniferous forests of Canada, but it responds readily to changes in the supply of cones by "irrupting"—moving south in large groups—when food is lacking. These irruptions tend to occur in alternate years, and they can involve many finch species, too, which also feed on conifers. Because the Red-breasted Nuthatch tends to move south before the finches do, it is an excellent indicator of more irruptions to follow and is known among birders as an "honorary finch."

It did not take long before I observed one. On Starr's first public walk of the fall, August 20, we were descending the path from Belvedere Castle past Turtle Pond when we both heard the familiar *yank-yank-yank* vocalization. We turned to each other and exclaimed "Red-breasted Nuthatch!" The trees were still fully-foliaged and we did not see the bird, nor would we see one for at least another week. With bird number 172 of the year, my fall was off to a great start.

The good momentum continued the following day with Starr in the North End, as we got clear views of a Philadelphia Vireo over the Pool. Starr had had this bird on a North End walk in the spring on a day when I was absent due to expected rain and cool conditions, so I was glad to finally complete my vireo collection for the year (Blue-headed, Red-eyed, Warbling, Yellow-throated, White-eyed, and Philadelphia). The Philadelphia Vireo is perhaps that hardest of all the vireos to observe because it does not have the piercing, distinctive call of the White-eyed nor the obvious plumage of the Yellow-throated. It can look a lot like the more common Warbling Vireo.

I figured that the Philadelphia Vireo would a tough bird for the other leading birders to get and for a long time it was. Anders Peltomaa wrote to me after I reported it to ask for more details and then went to the Pool to chase it, but he "dipped" (birder parlance for "did not re-find it"). Within three weeks, however, both he and Farnsworth had gotten the bird. It seems I could build a lead only with birds observed outside of Central Park.

For over a week I did not have anything new. Then, just after 8 a.m. on August 31, Jacob Drucker sent out a text alert regarding Red Crossbills he had briefly heard and seen flying overhead on the Lake. I had the species in mind even before Drucker's alert because an online post two days beforehand had mentioned that these finches were moving through northeastern states. I did not expect them to arrive this quickly.

I walked out to the Ramble after 9 a.m., not expecting to re-find a small flock of crossbills that by now could have moved entirely through the park, but wanting to be in the area just in case they reappeared. At 9:48 a.m. Anders Peltomaa issued a text alert that he had re-found the Red Crossbills in the hemlocks of Shakespeare Garden but that they had quickly flown out. I was just a couple hundred yards away near the Upper Lobe.

I decided the best strategy was to search the surrounding co-nifers in and around the Pinetum. If the Crossbills had flown *out* of the Shakespeare Garden, I saw little point to searching there.

I was wrong. At 10:13 Peltomaa again text-alerted to say that the Crossbills had returned to the Shakespeare Garden hemlocks within minutes and were still being seen. I bolted over and was the first to arrive. The Red Crossbills, with their overlapping bills, were plainly visible on the nearby conifers and their *gyp-gyp-gyp* calls filled the air.

Red Crossbills are exceedingly rare in Central Park; they oc-cur maybe once or twice per decade in those years with strong finch irruptions and they had no prior eBird records in all of Manhattan.

It was a historic morning for birders, and soon dozens of them were coming to the Shakespeare Garden overlook. The Red Crossbills stayed in those trees for two days, allowing many to notch a life Central Park bird. I recalled those painful twenty

minutes when I thought I had missed the crossbills and was sat-
isfied with getting them, along with the crowd, and moving up
to 174 for the year. It was like finishing a bicycle race amongst a
peloton of hundreds—every rider gets the same time, just as every birder got this species. The standings were unchanged.

The early arrival of the Red Crossbills set expectations high
for further appearances of the same species and of other finches.
Yet no other Red Crossbills were reported in Central Park in the
following month.

I did start thinking about exceeding 190 birds for the year,
and these hopes were bolstered by a well-circulated analysis of
cone-crop conditions, *"Ron Pittaway's Winter Finch Forecast,"*
which was posted on eBird on September 20. These finches could
add another four or five likely species, and eBird suggested that
Boreal Owl was also possible. Fall was already looking like an
intense birding season.

30

NIGHTHAWK WATCHMAN

I was always thinking about new birds to add to my year list. The best ones were those that other birders were unlikely to get—perhaps because they were not aware of them or perhaps because they simply did not want to bother pursuing them. Unusual waterfowl off the southern tip of Manhattan in winter; the Wild Turkey of Battery Park; the Yellow-crowned Night-Heron of Randall's Island; and the shorebirds of Swindler Cove—these had been my best ideas, birds that separated me from the pack.

My best idea for the early fall was the Common Nighthawk. It was not a hawk at all, but rather a mid-size insectivore with long, pointed wings. The best thing about this bird, from my point of view, was that it rarely was seen during the day, when most birders would be birding. Rather, it appeared near dusk, swooping over lakes and lighted areas to catch insect prey and continuing to hunt into the night. It used to be a commonly-seen fall migrant, even visible over buildings near the park. Now it is much less common but still known to occur. I wanted to see one!

So, beginning on Sunday, August 26, I went out to the Great Lawn area roughly 45 minutes before sunset, at 6:45 p.m., and stood watch until after 8 p.m. when darkness set in. I also tried the Great Hill area on some evenings, a likely spot for a flyover. I saw birds, mostly high-flying Chimney Swifts, but no night-hawks.

After four evenings like this I was feeling frustrated. Prospect Park, well south of Central Park in Brooklyn, was getting numerous Common Nighthawks every evening in the same time period. Why was I not seeing any?

After more nighthawk-free evenings, I finally caught a break. Just before 7 p.m. on September 5, a text alert announced two Common Nighthawks over the southeast end of the Lake. I was already in my running clothes, so I picked up my binoculars and ran toward the Ramble. I stopped at Turtle Pond first because I wanted to make sure the alerter had not mistaken it for the Lake. Turtle Pond had been a popular hunting place for Common Nighthawks some years ago.

Not seeing any overhead, I raced further into the Ramble to the Riviera, where I could not get a good view. I continued on to Bow Bridge, and suddenly two swooping birds with white-striped, angular wings came into view—Common Nighthawks! I followed them for another five minutes as they floated south and out of range. I did not see any other birders nearby. Perhaps this would be the unique sighting for which I had been hoping?

It turned out to be just that. Though Farnsworth had seen one over Sutton Place on August 30 (he had Common Nighthawks every year), none of the other leading birders reported this one or any others in the following days.

I had remedied another deficiency the day before in the North End, where I finally had an Olive-sided Flycatcher while birding with Lenore Swenson. Speaking of flycatchers, I spotted a Yellow-bellied Flycatcher with Starr on August 29, a species I had had in the spring but without a diagnostic view of my own. This one was clear, and Starr agreed.

Now I had reached 176 birds, eight up on Farnsworth and seventeen up on Peltomaa. If I could maintain this lead for the remaining two months of fall migration, the big year title almost surely would be mine.

31

WHIP-POOR-WILL

As the fall season moved along I was concerned about Starr. She had ably led the first three walks of August, but after that she had a planned absence of two walks during chemotherapy. Then, after returning to lead one walk in the Ramble, she missed the next four as Lenore Swenson filled in.

After that, when Starr began a walk, she was able to continue for only an hour or sometimes less.

It made sense that Starr had a tough time on hot days during chemotherapy, but now the pattern had changed for the worse: she also was weak even on cool days during breaks from chemo, which was never the case before. I believed that it was now the cancer making her weaker and not just the treatment, and this did not bode well.

My big year continued apace. Since spring I had been waiting to get the elusive Yellow-billed Cuckoo, but I always arrived too late, whether the report was from the Great Hill or from the Loch. The frustration ended on September 7 when an alert was sent from the Maintenance Meadow at 8:25 a.m. I ran for it right away; when I arrived, Joe DiCostanzo's group was also looking. Joe spotted the bird, number 177 for me, low in a crabapple tree.

I was planning on going directly to Starr's walk on the morning of Monday, September 10, but I received a 7:26 a.m. alert from eBird that Andrew Farnsworth had just observed Bobolink in good numbers on the Hudson at the West 72nd Street Pier.

BirdCast, for which Farnsworth writes, had warned that Bobolink were on the way and might be observed near dawn in the area, so I was prepared for them to show up.

Bobolink, which can resemble sparrows, are not rare in general but are extremely rare in New York City. These grassland birds migrate over Manhattan twice annually, but it seems that they almost never touch down. Starr Saphir, in over 30 years of birding Central Park, has had Bobolink only four or five times. Reports of them on eBird are few, and many of these belong to Farnsworth.

I ran out to the Hudson by 8:10 a.m., but I did not see any Bobolinks or even any passerine flocks at all. After returning and birding the Ramble with Starr, I wrote to Farnsworth to ask about his morning observations.

He explained that he had seen migrating flocks of Bobolink high overhead and had also heard their flight calls (which are, in general, different from calls made on land). He encouraged me to look for the Bobolink flocks as if I were raptor-watching: looking very high for small specks. He heard more flying over Belvedere Castle later that morning.

I went out to the Hudson even earlier (7:24 a.m.) the next morning, but again I did not see any passerine flocks. I really wanted the Bobolink, as it almost certainly would be observed by no one else. (And it wasn't.) But I had been too late on the best day for them. Even if I had seen some high-flying passerines, I doubt that I could have identified them as Bobolink with confidence. Farnsworth's knowledge of flight calls and his willingness to be on the Hudson at 6:45 a.m. allowed him to get a species that I would end up missing.

My day of birding, however, was just getting started. September 10 brought a massive raptor migration, specifically Sharp-shinned Hawk, which I needed for the year, and Broad-winged Hawk, which I was glad to see again as my spring sighting was less-than-optimal. Hundreds of Broad-winged Hawks, mostly flying in large flocks known as "kettles," filled the late-afternoon skies over Central Park. I observed these raptors from my favorite Central Park spot, aside or on the Great Lawn, as this gives a view in all directions unobstructed by trees.

The other place I like to go for raptor migration is Riverside Park south of 96th Street. This area is close to two geographic features that migrating raptors like to follow: the Hudson River to the west and the ridge marked by Broadway across Manhattan to the east. On the afternoon of the 15th I saw my first Bald Eagle of the year soaring over the Hudson.

Bald Eagles are rarely reported in Manhattan, but they are not really rare at all. I ended up seeing at least four during the fall. Though I had a couple over Central Park, I believe that Riverside Park is the better local choice, owing to its proximity to the Hudson River. Inwood Hill Park by the Dyckman Street ball fields and Fort Tryon Park are even better still (they are further north, also by the Hudson and on an even higher ridge line off of which raptors can catch rising air currents) and a great choice if you happen to live nearby.

The key to seeing Bald Eagles is actively raptor-watching, scanning the skies with binoculars, and doing so on days with favorable meteorological conditions in the fall or winter. The best days are those with northerly or northwesterly winds, preferably after the passage of a cold front, and with clear or partly-cloudy skies and no precipitation. On such days Bald Eagles should be visible almost daily over the Hudson.

Earlier that same day, at 9:48 a.m. on September 15, all Central

Park birders received a gift bird: an Eastern Whip-poor-will was found in a tree just above the source of the Gill. As I was running there, Starr called me to make sure I knew about it. She was always looking out for me. I arrived within ten minutes, and already two dozen birders were peering at it.

The Eastern Whip-poor-will is very rare in Central Park and not observed every year, though it is likely that every year at least one such bird passes through. The problem is that these birds are quiet and largely motionless during the day, and their plumage allows them to blend in almost perfectly with tree branches so that they look like bumps of bark. This is how they avoid being attacked by Cooper's Hawks while they are sleeping and defenseless. They tend not to draw the attention of Blue Jays and crows, making them much harder to find even than owls.

After getting my views of the bird, I called Starr back to let her and the group know exactly where to find it. It turned out that she had quit the walk well before calling me and had already gone back to her home in Inwood. This meant that Lenore Swenson and the group almost certainly did not know about the bird—Lenore still had not gotten a cell phone. So I ran to the North End, found her by the Meer, and told everyone the good news. Lenore made a special trip to the Ramble after her walk was done so that her group could see the whip-poor-will.

This bird would amaze all by remaining in the same area, even mostly on the same branch, for at least four days.

My total had grown to 180 birds for the year. I was eight up on Farnsworth, who also had a Bald Eagle that same day, and twenty up on Peltomaa as of September 15.

32

A TALE OF TWO WARBLERS

2012 in Manhattan was a remarkable year for observing the very rarest warblers. Those readers who want a thorough analysis of the relative abundance of the 36 warblers that regularly occur here, along with a recap of when and where the rarest spring warblers were observed, are encouraged to examine the Appendix at the back of this book and then return here.

In this chapter I want to discuss two of these warblers, Connecticut Warbler and Golden-winged Warbler. They appear here mostly in the fall migration season, though they have sometimes occurred in spring, too. Both usually are reported at least once in Central Park each year but sometimes only once. They are two of the most difficult of all warblers for local birders to observe.

The first report of Connecticut Warbler came from Anthony Collerton on the morning of Tuesday, September 4, near the Upper Lobe in the Ramble. Collerton would go on to set a New York State big year record in 2012 with 361 species.

I had been at home getting ready to bird with Lenore's group in the North End when I received the bird alert. I ran fast, with a life bird on the line. When I arrived, birders had already gathered to search the triangular patch of trees and brush just north of the Upper Lobe. Collerton told me he had seen it clearly but briefly and that he had also observed it walking (as opposed to hopping), which distinguished the species from similar birds such as the Common Yellowthroat.

I circled the area more than a few times and was joined by Joe DiCostanzo's Natural History group. The bird was never re-found.

Another Connecticut was reported, too late to chase, in the Loch on Saturday, September 8. Oddly, the report time suggests that I was nearby with Lenore's group and probably passed by within 15 minutes of the sighting.

Yet another was reported near the Maintenance Meadow early on the 16th but not until hours after the sighting.

On the morning of Monday, September 17, I decided to skip the 7:30 a.m. walk in the Ramble with Starr. I had been birding many days straight and wanted to take a break while staying ready to chase rarities. In retrospect, I am glad I did, because just after 9 a.m. a text alert announced a Connecticut Warbler being observed on the south lawn of Bryant Park in midtown. I went directly to the East 86th Street subway station and took the train to Grand Central. From there I ran Bryant Park, which is just west of the New York Public Library.

I saw a few other birders watching the lawn, which at the time was closed to walkers and so was a large, undisturbed foraging area for a number of Common Yellowthroats and a trimmer warbler, walking, with a brown/gray hood, a longer bill, and an eye-ring: the Connecticut!

I called to alert Starr, who had seen an excellent bird of her own in the Ramble (a Rufous Hummingbird). Then I took some long looks at the Connecticut and left the park.

I was glad that I had not delayed in chasing the Connecticut (why would anyone delay in chasing a Connecticut?) because sometime around 10 a.m. the Bryant Park lawn was opened to foot traffic, and the Connecticut quickly took to hiding in the planters. Those who arrived later had to wait nearly two hours for the bird to make another brief appearance.

Manhattan birding in 2012 was all about multiple opportunities, however, and even those who missed this sighting would get an even better chance. On Sunday morning, September 23, around 10:30, a Connecticut Warbler was reported in Tupelo Meadow. I ran out to see it, but it was no longer being seen and after some searching I decided to head to the Pool in the North End, where a Marsh Wren had been reported the previous day. I again failed to observe the Marsh Wren, but another text alert said the Connecticut had been re-found. I ran back to Tupelo Meadow and at 11:50 I saw at least 30 birders lining the fenced-in area just north of the meadow. Within five minutes the Connecticut walked briefly into view only 25 feet away.

This Connecticut was by far the most cooperative one of all. It lingered in the same brushy area the entire day, allowing dozens of birders to see it.

Another Connecticut appeared at the Oval in Stuyvesant Town on the 25th and continued for at least five days.

As for the Golden-winged Warbler, even though Prospect Park in Brooklyn had almost daily reports of it in late August, it was still very hard to get in Central Park.

On September 19 a 7:15 a.m. text alert told of a Golden-winged Warbler at Strawberry Fields. I was just getting ready to run to Lenore's walk, which would start only seven blocks north. I intercepted Lenore on the way there, told the group about the Golden-winged, and then continued running.

Once again, I arrived to find that the bird was no longer being seen. There were plenty of other warblers, though, for the twenty or so birders to see: Magnolia, Black-and-White, Black-throated Green, Northern Parula, and, best of all, a Tennessee. Five Rose-breasted Grosbeaks and a Brown Thrasher also appeared. Lenore's group arrived, and we continued to get birds for over an hour there, but no one re-found the Golden-winged. I walked home.

At 4:05 p.m. an online alert said that the Golden-winged Warbler had returned. I ran to Strawberry and encountered the birders who had reported it. Once again, it was no longer being seen! I wished the birders had been quicker to report it, as my ten-minute transit time was not to blame.

Jeffrey Kimball soon arrived. He was an accomplished birder himself, and he had spent years in the park filming migrants to get just the right views and sounds for his film. He and I scanned all the trees as the shadows grew longer, but we did not find what we wanted.

Around 5 p.m. Anders Peltomaa and others arrived. Kimball had to leave for an event, but now we had roughly ten birders on the prowl. Since the bird had been seen there at various times since early this morning, we thought it might possibly still be around.

I was getting tired of looking, but I remembered the mistake I made last year in giving up too early on the Rufous Hummingbird. As long as other birders remained, so would I.

At 5:45 one of the birders thought it might have popped up briefly behind trees along the dirt path running across the eastern edge of the hilltop. I focused my attention near a particular tree where I was seeing some movement, and fifteen minutes later I got a brief but diagnostic view of it: yellow wing patch, yellow crown, and white stripes above the eye and extending from the bill, with a dark gray mask and throat—a female Golden-winged Warbler!

I called out to Anders that I had seen it, and he said that he had, too. A long day of birding was finally over. With bird number 182 I had completed my observations of the entire 36 regularly-occurring warblers in Manhattan in a single year. I walked home across the park, hungry and tired, but proud of having achieved a rare feat.

While other Manhattanites were marketing products, creating software, or dispensing legal advice, I was running around the park in my shorts and singlet, trying to encounter as many species of birds as I could. Ten years ago I would have laughed at the thought of taking a break from managing hedge funds to look for rare birds. Devoting two years to such a quest—doubly crazy! But I had accepted the challenge, and there was no turning back now, not with the big year lead in hand.

Andrew Farnsworth had a Golden-winged Warbler himself by Belvedere Castle the next day. There was just no stopping him! Another appeared before several birders in the Maintenance Meadow on October 1.

33

CHASING THE CLAY-COLORED SPARROW

After getting the Connecticut and Golden-winged Warblers, I felt much more strongly positioned to go on for the big year win. I had observed all the species I could reasonably expect to find— so far—in Central Park. More would be on the way soon: irruptive finches, Red-shouldered Hawks, Golden Eagles, and some unusual ducks. For now, though, long birding walks in the park offered little reward. It was time to rest, tend to other responsibilities, and continue monitoring the alerts.

One rarity that I no longer needed to chase was the American Bittern, which was reported late on Sunday, September 10, after being seen in the reeds of Turtle Pond. It was then seen again and for nearly a week beginning on the 12th in the same area, sometimes in trees and other times well-hidden on the shore of the pond's island. Central Park birders had no excuse for missing this scarce species, which also had a well-reported appearance in the North Woods during the spring, when I saw it.

An alert I *did* need to chase arrived the same week, late in the afternoon on September 12. Nadir Souirgi, who regularly birded the North End, had learned from another birder of a Clay-colored Sparrow in the Loch. Nadir himself later relocated the bird associating with House Sparrows at the northwest end of the Compost Heap at 4:30 p.m., when he reported it.

I ran over and surveyed the scene. I saw House Sparrows but no Clay-colored. Soon Nadir arrived and said that he thought the bird had flown east to the other end of the heap. We checked there and still did not find it. Further searching that afternoon also proved fruitless.

The next day, just after noon, Nadir posted online that the Clay-colored had been seen in the Loch at 7 a.m. by a very reliable birder. So I again visited the North End in the late afternoon and looked around the Rustic Bridge where it was supposed to have been. Again I did not find it.

Late that night Nadir posted that he had *again* seen the Clay-colored by the Rustic Bridge, just a little later than I had checked it, from 6 p.m. to 7 p.m. That would have been a good time for him to send another text alert! The Clay-colored was becoming my new white whale (I have had many of these, as you know by now, some of which remain at large to this day).

It would get worse. On Sunday morning, September 16, I was raptor-watching in Riverside Park near 90th Street. Matthew Rymkiewicz alerted that he had just seen the Clay-colored Sparrow on the southern slope of the Great Hill in the North End. I was about ten minutes late in noticing the alert because I had not heard my cell beep when it arrived. It took me another ten minutes to run to the Great Hill, where I saw neither the birder nor the bird. Another half-hour of searching did not reward me.

I knew that this bird was around, but I was not seeing it. I could not get it out of my mind. After returning home and having lunch, I decided later in the afternoon go for it again. I ran to the Great Hill and examined the slope that had produced so many great sparrow sightings over the years, including Lark Sparrow last year. I had a Red-eyed Vireo, a Brown Thrasher, an

Eastern Kingbird, and my first-of-season Palm Warbler and Eastern Phoebe. I did not have the Clay-colored Sparrow.

On the morning of September 20 I was at home when a 10:45 a.m. text alert announced the Clay-colored was being seen at the Grassy Knoll. I ran there and was fortunate to encounter the couple who had reported it. They quickly got me on the bird. There was no doubt that it was a Clay-colored Sparrow—it had a buffy breast and pale lores, which distinguished it from its more common look-alike, the Chipping Sparrow.

The Clay-colored Sparrow had been reported thus far by only one other eBird user, and I thought it would put me further ahead of Farnsworth, who got nearly all of his birds in Sutton Place and did not regularly respond to text alerts from Central Park. I got to enjoy my incremental lead for exactly one day. Then Farnsworth visited the park on the 21st and tallied 56 species, including the Clay-colored Sparrow, in nearly four hours of birding.

I had 183 birds now to his 178—only a five-bird lead, the closest it had been in months. Everyone else was twenty or more birds back.

There had been another species on my mind lately: Marsh Wren. Tom Fiore, one of Central Park's most highly-regarded birders, had reported one online on the 21st and 22nd, first in the North End's Wildflower Meadow (an improbable place to find one) and then on the nearby shore of the Pool, but his posts came many hours after his observations and my belated attempts at chasing failed.

The Marsh Wren is reported only once or twice per year in Central Park, though it is not in general a rare bird. Its preferred habitat is cattail marshes, where it nests. Since these are in short supply in Central Park, we get the species only as it passes through in migration, and it tends not to linger.

As I was walking the Ramble with Lenore Swenson on the

morning of the 24th, another birder told us of a Marsh Wren sighting nearby in Tupelo Meadow, in the fenced-in area east of the Tupelo tree. It took at least a half-hour of searching before anyone in our group saw it, as the thick, weedy vegetation gave it cover. The species tends to call frequently and distinctively, but it was staying silent. Eventually it wandered to the northwest edge of the fence line where Al Levantin and I saw it briefly.

Marsh Wrens surprised birders by appearing often again: once at the Meer the next day, once in the Maintenance Meadow on September 29, and once in Bryant Park on October 6.

Three noteworthy birds that I had already had were reported in late September. A Dickcissel was seen on the 21st in the Wildflower Meadow and later near the Compost Heap. I tried for it that day—it would have been my first in Central Park, but I could not re-find it. A Blue Grosbeak was seen late on the afternoon of the 25th, also in the Wildflower Meadow. A Grasshopper Sparrow was seen by many, and for most of the day, on the 29th around the Compost Heap.

The Marsh Wren, species number 184 of the year, was the last new bird I would get for over two weeks. After Farnsworth added a White-crowned Sparrow, which I had observed in February, my lead was again cut to just five birds as September came to a close.

34

RARITIES OF RANDALL'S ISLAND

By the time October begins, warblers, vireos, and tanagers have already had their peak weeks ago and are now being seen less and less often. Thrushes are still abundant but declining in numbers. Sparrows and raptors, however, are just beginning their ascent to peak abundance—the former in mid-October and the latter in early November.

This year, October birders also had another group on their minds: the finches. The early arrival of Red Crossbills on August 31 was starting to look more like a tease rather than a harbinger of things to come. No more crossbills had been observed in Central Park since those first ones departed, nor had any other new finches appeared.

This would quickly change, as reports of small numbers of Pine Siskins appeared online beginning October 2. I chased these the next two days in the Wildflower Meadow, but I observed only House Finches and American Goldfinches.

Pine Siskins are small, brown, streaked birds that have a few distinguishing features: a slim, pointed bill; often some yellow on the wings; and a harsh, rising trill call. They like thistle feeders, just as American Goldfinches do, but it would take until much later in the season for visiting Pine Siskins to find and use the feeders in Evodia Field. I would have to do some foot work to find these birds.

A more promising report came on Friday the Fifth, as a number of people had seen Pine Siskins in the dawn redwoods at the north end of Strawberry Fields. The species prefers the seeds of conifers, which are not abundant in the Ramble, so it made sense that these birds would first visit some of the highest and most prominent conifers in the park.

I scanned the redwoods for them on the afternoon of the Fifth and again midday on Sixth, but they did not reappear.

When I read on Sunday the Seventh of a very large Pine Siskin flight observed over Montauk, I started to become concerned that the species may have been mostly flying over or around Central Park. There were too few of them being observed, and they did not appear to be lingering. I could tell from the density of observations to the north of New York City on eBird that there would be enough Pine Siskins to eventually produce a sighting, but I did not like seeing five days pass from their initial appearance in Central Park without my logging at least one. With the big year lead came some standards to uphold, even if these were only in my mind!

On Monday, October 8, Lenore's walk in the Ramble went well—51 species, including another Blue Grosbeak in the Maintenance Meadow, but no Pine Siskins.

By this point we were seeing plenty of Black-capped Chickadees, a bird I was able only to hear in the spring, so I was glad to be able to report this species more definitively with both sight and sound.

With light rain expected to fall, I did not go on the North End walk on Tuesday the Ninth. This was just as well, because at 9:50 a.m. I received a text alert of a large flock of Pine Siskins, roughly 50, moving through the Upper Lobe. I figured a flock this size would be hard to miss, and I ran toward the Ramble. On the way, just east of the Great Lawn, I saw a flock of small brown birds quickly moving from tree to tree and emitting sharp trills. As I looked more closely, I could tell it was the Pine Siskins! Finally I had gotten them.

I would get them many more times in October all over the park. My two-week drought had ended with bird number 185.

Now I could turn my attention back to raptor- and sparrow-watching. It would take only three days for me to get the last relatively easy raptor that I needed. Just after lunch on the 12th I went out to the Great Lawn to scan the skies. I saw a great variety of raptors: twenty-six Turkey Vultures, which would end up being my highest one-day total of the species for the year; six Cooper's Hawks; two Sharp-shinned Hawks; six Red-tailed Hawks; and one Red-shouldered Hawk, a bird that circled the Great Lawn, giving excellent low-altitude views, and became species number 186 for the year.

Speaking of hawks, the Red-tailed Hawk is by far the most abundant hawk in Central Park. Red-tails famously nest on tall buildings adjacent to the park and elsewhere in the city. See the excellent *Urban Hawks* site for the latest photos and stories. It is easy to see at least one Red-tailed Hawk nearly every time you visit the park.

The Cooper's Hawk is the next most common, less than a third as abundant as the Red-tailed, and generally observed only in the fall and winter months.

The Sharp-shinned Hawk, an *accipiter* just like the Cooper's and very similar in appearance to it, is the third most common hawk in the park. It is present in small numbers throughout the winter and spring, absent during the summer, and seen in greatest abundance during October migration.

The Broad-winged Hawk and the Red-shouldered Hawk, both *buteos* like the Red-tailed Hawk, are scarce during all times of the year except fall migration. They are almost always nonresident hawks just passing through. The time to see the Broad-winged is early to mid-September; for the Red-shouldered, mid-October to early November.

These last two hawks call to mind a principle that has guided me throughout my big year: for every species there is an optimal time of the year to observe it. You need to look at the data—eBird is excellent for this purpose—and figure out what this time is. You also need to think about what the best location is. In a place like Manhattan with so many dedicated birders, you could get away with just watching the boards and eBird to see what is being reported and then going out to get it. But if you understand the timing of migration along with how weather patterns affect it, you can plan your birding intelligently and use your time and energy where the reward is greatest.

That said, when you see the report of a needed rarity, you have to go for it. On the evening of Saturday, October 13, Alan Drogin sent out an online post that would ignite interest in Randall's Island, a place that had received little attention from most Manhattan birders. He had wandered north that day after an organized walk through the restored saltmarsh to check out the northern shore of the island, a place that he occasionally birded. Less than a month ago he had reported a Black-headed Gull there, a sighting I did not chase because I believed the odds were too low that the bird would return.

This time, while observing a Bonaparte's Gull at low tide (an excellent sighting in its own right), he noticed "three Nelson's Sharp-tailed Sparrows munching on top of the saltmarsh grass." He eventually counted five such sparrows, four of which he believed to be the Atlantic subspecies and one, the Interior (with better-defined streaks). The location: right across from the backstop of baseball field #42.

Nelson's Sparrows are of the *Ammodramus* genus, as are Grasshopper Sparrows. *Ammodramus* sparrows, of which there are seven species appearing in the eastern United States, are exceedingly scarce in Manhattan and are not observed every year. The last reported appearance of a Nelson's Sparrow in Manhattan had been in Central Park in 2002. Nelson's Sparrows prefer coastal saltmarsh habitats, and very few parts of Manhattan qualify as such.

The next morning I got a late start, but by 10:50 a.m. I had taken the subway to East 125th Street and run across the RFK Bridge to Randall's Island. I then ran north to the Bronx Kill, where I had seen Killdeer over the summer, and started walking east toward the baseball field #42 area. A Lincoln's Sparrow provided a good sighting along the way.

I expected to see a crowd of birders gathered around, but there were none. For at least a short while, I would have the location all to myself.

As I approached the rocks by the shore, I saw a perching sparrow. I raised my binoculars and saw it clearly but briefly before it scurried away. It was one of the Nelson's Sparrows!

I walked out onto the rocks, searching the reeds, but I could not relocate it.

Then, turning my attention to the opposite shore of the Kill, I saw the perching Bonaparte's Gulls. Their ear-spots, black bills, and size—little more than half that of the nearby Herring Gulls—made identification easy.

Out of the corner of my eye I detected movement on the nearby reeds. A new bird had arrived—a Marsh Wren! My view of it was close and unobstructed, far better than what I had in Tupelo Meadow the previous month.

I wanted to see more Nelson's Sparrows, but they were not appearing. Perhaps my presence was making them cautious. I decided to leave for a bit and examine the rest of the shore.

As I walked east I saw more Savannah Sparrows than I had ever seen before, ten or so, along with some Song Sparrows. Clearly this coastal spot offered a mix of birds far different from that of Central Park.

When I returned to my initial location, I soon saw two Nelson's Sparrows clearly at close range. They had blurry gray streaks on their breasts, making them the Atlantic variety.

This was enough for me—I had observed the two species I wanted (Bonaparte's Gull and Nelson's Sparrow), and waiting for the Interior subspecies to show up would not change my total.

I headed home and entered my observations into eBird. I was amazed that no one else reported from Randall's Island that Sunday. These sparrows had not been noted in Manhattan in nine years!

Other birders arrived on Monday, including Farnsworth, and soon word spread on the message boards and everyone wanted to have a look at these sparrows.

The sharper-streaked one that Drogin had labeled an Interior subspecies of Nelson's led to much debate online as more photos were taken and distributed. Some believed it might be a hybrid Nelsons/Sharp-tailed Sparrow.

I left this debate to the professional ornithologists. Hybrids do not count toward species totals, so even if it is was one it would not do me any good.

Reports of other rarities soon brought me back to the area behind backstop #42. First was a Green-winged Teal, which Farnsworth observed early on the morning of October 17. I visited the next day and did not see one.

Next was a Vesper Sparrow, reported there on the 21st while the birder was looking for the Nelson's Sparrows. I had the species last year in the North End but not yet this year. It is very rare and not observed every year in Central Park.

I made three more visits to Randall's Island in October to try for the Vesper Sparrow, but I did not get it. I also worked the North End, where it had appeared in previous years, but to no avail.

I made one of those visits to Randall's Island at 8:15 a.m. on October 23. I was excited to see an abundance of Savannah Sparrows, close to 20, along the north shore. This species is seen uncommonly, usually in very small numbers, in Central Park. I also had Lincoln's Sparrow, White-crowned Sparrow, and Swamp Sparrow. I even had a couple Pine Siskins. These were good birds but not the ones I wanted.

I ran south through the island and over the 103rd Street pedestrian bridge back to Manhattan, and from there I ran to the North End of Central Park to meet up with Lenore and her group around 10 a.m. I told her about my excellent sparrow observations, and then she one-upped me: about 15 minutes ago she had found an American Tree Sparrow on the south slope of the Great Hill.

The American Tree Sparrow looks much like a Field Sparrow, another member of the *Spizella* genus, but it has a bicolored bill and a dark spot on the center of its breast. It is common over much of the rest of the country (particularly the interior states) but rarely seen in Central Park, though it is a regular visitor, in small numbers, in the late fall and winter.

Lenore gave me good directions, and I went to search for it. Generally sparrows on the Great Hill are easy to re-find. They associate with other similar sparrows to form a flock, and the flock is easy enough to notice even though it may move around.

This American Tree Sparrow had been seen with Chipping Sparrows, which also belong to *Spizella*. I saw plenty of them, along with Juncos, but forty minutes of searching did not produce the tree sparrow.

Although it made sense for me to have gone to Randall's Island, which potentially offered a variety of birds that I needed, it irked me that by simply having shown up for the 9 a.m. North End walk I could have had one more bird! My thoughts fixated on the American Tree Sparrow, just as they had on the Clay-colored Sparrow. I returned to the Great Hill the next day and again left without success.

Meanwhile, the debate over the Nelson's Sparrows continued to boil. New evidence was revealed: one of the sparrows responded to a Saltmarsh Sparrow call and not to a Nelson's Sparrow call. Photos suggested that a sparrow different from the original ones may have arrived. I was not sure, but I could not afford to risk missing a new species, so I made sure to observe these sparrows again and get a glimpse of the one with the crispest gray streaks. I entered it as a hybrid Nelson's/Saltmarsh, which was the conservative thing to do and in line with Farnsworth's thinking.

On October 28 Jacob Drucker observed it and was sure it was a pure Saltmarsh and not a hybrid. Other birders agreed, and a consensus was swiftly reached. I revised my listing to reflect this newfound accord, gaining one more species in the process.

The northeast shore of Randall's Island had quickly become *the* place to find bird species unavailable elsewhere. Soon even more casual birders were making the trip. I was proud to have been the first eBird user to regularly cover the island in July 2012. It would continue to produce remarkable finds throughout the rest of the year.

I had gotten three new birds at Randall's Island in October, raising my total to 189, which was near what I expected for my entire year just three months ago. With only a couple weeks left in the fall migration season before the bird spigot was shut off, I should have been in prime position to take it easy and let the calendar run out. Instead, I was in trouble—big trouble.

35

A STORM IS BREWING

Andrew Farnsworth was on a tear. I was six birds up on him after both of us had gotten the Nelson's Sparrows and the Bonaparte's Gull as of October 18.

On Sunday the 21st he added two birds that I had expected him to get, Red-shouldered Hawk and Eastern Bluebird—the latter a bit early, though. His third bird, however, was a megararity: Northern Goshawk.

Northern Goshawk is the largest and rarest of the three *accipiters* that occur in the eastern United States. It breeds in Canadian forests and only rarely ventures as far south as Manhattan (except in the western states, where it may appear in Arizona and New Mexico). It can be distinguished from the other *accipiters* by color (gray, if it is an adult) and otherwise by its broader body and more pointed wing shape. It had only a few eBird records in Manhattan, the earliest dating back to 1997.

Farnsworth immediately shared information on the sighting with text alerts, but he had observed it from his apartment and it was already well past my uptown address, flying high enough that he needed to use his scope to make the identification. I could not reasonably expect to get another one, even if I spent hours watching the skies each day.

Farnsworth soon struck again with another difficult species. On October 24 he observed several American Woodcock calling as they flew over his building after 10:40 p.m. What could I do? I am not even allowed to go on my building's sixth-floor roof, and I do not live on a flyway. I could listen from the Great Lawn or Belvedere Castle for woodcocks flying over at night, but I was already spending my days pursuing birds and there was still a chance of encountering a woodcock on the ground.

The American Woodcock does appear in the fall in Central Park—reported usually just once—but it tends to flush when it is discovered, so that woodcock alerts, if there actually were any, would be useless. The bird flies away too fast.

Occasionally a woodcock will show up somewhere in mid-town where it can be viewed easily as it is overwhelmed by the tall buildings and traffic and frozen in place. Jacob Drucker found an American Woodcock sitting on a New York Public Library window sill on January 6 when he was birding Bryant Park. Opportunities like this, of course, cannot be counted upon.

Now, as of October 24, Farnsworth had 186 birds to my 188. He was gaining on me with birds I most likely could not match.

Farnsworth had begun his rally in September with the Bobolink and continued it with Snow Goose and Green-winged Teal in October. I could not believe I was still missing the latter two, which are regular visitors to the park—Snow Goose in flyovers, and Green-winged Teal on any of the large bodies of water. None of the other leading birders had them either, but this was little consolation.

In addition to Farnsworth's unanswerable scoring, another mid-month birding incident had left me rattled. After sunset on October 17, a Long-eared Owl was reported to have been in Central Park. The person reporting it noted that, according to the rules of the message board (NYSBirds), he could not disclose the specific location. Worse yet, later that evening an eBird report arrived indicating that the owl had been observed in the early afternoon, around 2:30 p.m., and for over two hours—plenty of time to send out some sort of notice, even if only a general one, such as "Long-eared Owl in Central Park," which would have been allowed on either message board. Yet no one did.

I went out to the Pinetum that evening to listen for it. The Pinetum was just a guess; Long-eared Owls prefer to roost in pines and what better place to find pines than the Pinetum? I did not hear it.

The next day, new info arrived on eBird: one of the observers wrote that the owl had been seen in a holly tree. Right away I knew the location of the sighting: Strawberry Fields, one of only a few places in the park with such trees. I went there and looked around, listening for Blue Jays to harass the owl and give away its location.

Though I observed no Blue Jay mobbing, I did notice a couple of birders passing along the trail and looking up at one of the holly trees and scanning it carefully for minutes with their binoculars. Confirmation!

Indeed, I later learned, this is where the owl had been. Today it no longer was there, and I did not find it at other owl-friendly locations in the park.

It was a huge missed opportunity for me but nothing more, as none of the other top birders on the eBird list had seen it, either. At least that is what I thought until *a week later* when one of them submitted a report of a Long-eared Owl sighting on the 17th. I was furious!

Long-eared Owls appear in the park not quite every year and almost always in the middle of winter when they do. When heavy snow to the north covers their hunting grounds, they fly south in groups in search of better conditions. This is likely what brought several of them to Central Park in February 2011, my first (and last) observation of the species. I would probably not get another chance to see one until next year.

This incident just made me more determined to increase my lead by finding other birds.

It also called to mind a debate that had raged earlier in the year on the birding boards: was it right to report the roosting locations of owls? Both eBirdsNYC and NYSBirds list owners strongly discouraged it. Those against point out that large numbers of observers can stress the owl, perhaps by approaching it too closely, and cause it to leave its roost and be found more easily by predators; or the owl can simply be deprived of adequate daytime rest.

This argument would carry more weight if bird alerts went out to everyone in New York, but they do not—they go out to birders dedicated enough to subscribe to them. I have never seen Central Park birders mistreat an owl.

On the other hand, I have seen Central Park *birds* mistreat owls often! Blue Jays, American Crows, and Red-tailed Hawks love to harass owls, which they see as threats. This loud harassment (and it is almost always just that, cawing and screeching with no physical contact) is actually how most owls are found by birders. This is something with which owls have to deal no matter where they are.

In nearly all cases, owls (other than Northern Saw-whet) roost high enough and with sufficient tree coverage that humans could not possibly be seen as a threat. As for the large crowds that can form around owls, these often consist mostly of passersby, *not* birders. People seeing even a few birders intently looking at something will approach and want to find out what is so interesting. This is unavoidable, whether a bird alert is sent out or not. The best solution, which had been implemented in the previous Long-eared Owl appearance, is to have a park ranger with a scope keeping everyone at a safe distance and offering views to those who show up without binoculars so that no one is tempted to move in too close.

As I see it, alerting all local birders to an owl's location would do little to bother the owl in most cases while bringing much joy and satisfaction to the many people who care about these birds. I accept that there are instances where an owl chooses a low, exposed roost that can be viewed only from nearby, and then it is right to ensure the owl's safety by not broadcasting its location. I certainly do not want to see owls, or any sensitive species, harmed by excessive human curiosity.

You might think that those opposed to more public alerts of owls would, in principle, stay away when word leaks out, as it often does, of an owl in the park. Ha! Of course not—they go out and see the owl. Then they call or text their friends to come and see it, so it is a matter of who is in "club owl."

The eBird site handles owl reports more fairly and democratically. It relays quickly whatever information gets posted but advises its users to follow the ethical guidelines of the American Birding Association in choosing how precisely to give the location of sensitive species. It even provides an option for completely hiding lists from public reporting, which sometimes is desirable, such as when the bird is on your private land and you do not want crowds coming by. The best way to find where the owls (and other rare birds) are is to become an eBird user and then exercise good judgment in how you do your chasing.

People can, of course, post whatever they want on their own websites or in emails to other birders.

If you use one of the popular message boards, you can try to be as explicit and timely as possible without stepping over the line.

One lesson of the internet age is that information will get out.

At the end of October, New Yorkers had a much more pressing concern than owl reports: Hurricane Sandy was barreling up the

East Coast. Forecasters gave ample warning of the potential damage and flooding that was to ensue and New York City took unusual precautions ahead of time, shutting down all subways and buses as of 7 p.m. on Sunday, October 28, and even closing all New York City parks as of 5 p.m.

I did not plan to bird that day. It was overcast and windy, and I had already had all the species likely to be found in Central Park. I was thinking ahead to hurricane birding—learning about the unusual birds that the storm might bring.

I was therefore surprised when I read, just after 5 p.m., a 4:32 p.m. message board report of several Green-winged Teal having been seen on the Lake in the morning. I had been looking for these ducks—I needed them! Reporting them a half-hour before the park's closing was not doing anyone any good.

I had not gotten any text alerts on these ducks or on any other birds lately, and I began to wonder if I was missing messages. So I went to the website for the text alerts and saw that I had indeed missed some. I had switched cell phones recently, and, though I kept the same number, my address for texting from an email source surely had changed with my new provider. I had not recalled that the text alerts worked this way, so I had not thought to enroll my new phone.

The first couple messages I missed would not have been of interest, but the third one was. It had been sent at 4:58 p.m. that day: "Northern Saw-whet Owl at the Point."

I thought it had to be a prank, and a cruel one at that: post the sighting of an owl that every birder would want to see, just two minutes before the park closes. Who would even be birding in the park at that time to report it?

Nevertheless, I ran to the nearest park entrance at 79th and Fifth, and already barricades were in place. At 72nd and Fifth a crew of New York City police were making it clear to all that, no, you cannot go in the park. This was good enough for me. I turned around and ran home, figuring that there probably had not been an owl and, even if there had, no one else was going to get to see it.

Several hours later my assumption was proved wrong: I received an eBird report of a Northern Saw-whet Owl sighting at the Point that had been made by a reputable birder. Apparently, I later learned, the west side of the park had been guarded much less rigorously than the east side, and the birder managed to gain entry well after 5 p.m.

I knew that the park was likely to be closed for many days and this only added to my frustration! Up to now, Northern Saw-whet Owls had been exceedingly rare visitors to Central Park, appearing only a couple of times per decade and generally not staying long. I figured the storm would probably discourage the owl from leaving the park, but the park would likely stay closed for many days after the storm subsided (which it did), giving the owl plenty of time to exit unseen.

By missing these owls, my lead over the rest of the field (aside from Farnsworth) had fallen to sixteen birds. A lead of this size going into November would, in nearly all years, be extremely safe. But with a hurricane on the way, strange things could happen. Fifteen or more unusual species might pass quickly through the area, with little opportunity for chasing. Fortuitous timing and location choice could disproportionately favor one birder over another. I did not want to give anyone else a chance to get back in the game.

I already had my hands full with a charging Farnsworth, whose performance the previous year during Hurricane Irene showed that he was willing to go out in awful conditions, for hours on end, and get rare birds otherwise never seen in the area.

With everything going against me in the past two weeks, I felt that my big year luck had completely run out.

36

HURRICANE BIRDING

Birders get excited when they learn that a hurricane might pass nearby, and not just because of its awesome destructive power. A hurricane can offer land birders the chance to see faraway species that they otherwise might not encounter.

Hurricanes do this in two ways: 1) by entrainment—birds getting trapped in or near the eye and getting dragged along, possibly for hundreds of miles; and 2) by displacement—strong winds blowing birds in flight.

By October 26 it was clear that New York City was in the path of what would be the largest Atlantic hurricane on record. I prepared for it by following the usual recommendations—making sure I had many gallons of tap water stored (I refreshed my supply from Hurricane Irene of August 2011) along with plenty of non-perishable food and also by educating myself about the strange, new birds that might be showing up.

East Coast birders were kept exceptionally well-informed by the sites eBird and *BirdCast* (for which Andrew Farnsworth researches and writes), which explained in detail how hurricanes affected birds, what birds might be moved, and where and when to look for them.

I spent hours studying the information these sites provided

and learning to identify over twenty species that I otherwise never expected to see in Manhattan. My analysis below draws upon articles from eBird and *BirdCast*. I also reviewed the online birding reports from the previous year's Hurricane Irene.

According to eBird[1], the hurricane birds could come from a number of sources, of which the three most relevant for Manhattan were:

1) **Entrained tropical species:** these are birds that normally would be found in tropical waters. They would be among the most sought-after birds. Examples: White-tailed Tropicbird, Magnificent Frigatebird, and Royal Tern.

2) **Displaced pelagic species:** there are birds that spend entire seasons far out at sea but are pushed inland by strong winds. If you want to risk seasickness, you can go on so-called pelagic birding trips, generally lasting a day or so, and see these birds in person. Or you could just stay on land and wait for a hurricane. Among these birds are Leach's and Wilson's Storm-Petrel, Cory's Shearwater and other shearwaters, Pomarine and Parasitic Jaeger, Red Phalarope, and various alcids.

3) **Coastal displaced species:** these are birds that occur off of nearby coasts, such as those of southern Long Island, but are pushed inland by strong winds. Examples are Laughing Gull, Bonaparte's Gull, Northern Gannet, Forster's Tern, Royal Tern, Black Skimmer, and various ducks, such White-winged Scoter, Surf Scoter, Black Scoter, and Long-tailed Duck.

Hurricane Sandy's first effects in Manhattan were felt on Sun-

---

[1] "Hurricane Sandy Strategies," 31 October 2012, eBird.org.

day, October 28, as winds picked up and a light rain began to fall in the evening.

In private communication, Farnsworth had suggested that the best place to go birding would be the 70th Street Pier on the Hudson River. This is where many excellent sightings occurred during Irene, and this is where I planned to go on the morning of the 29th.

My arrival there was hastened by an 8:45 a.m. text alert from Jacob Drucker, who evidently was back in town and who had just seen some White-winged Scoters at the 79th Street Boat Basin.

I caught a cross-town bus and ran to Riverside Drive. There I encountered what would be the first of many obstacles to hurricane birding: yellow police tape stretched across the entrance to Riverside Park, with a reminder that the park was closed. I went to 79th Street and tried to use the entrance to the Boat Basin off the bridge, but police tape was also blocking it. So I continued south and finally found a path that did not have any yellow tape. I took it to the Hudson Greenway, a narrow, paved running/bicycling path directly adjacent to the Hudson River.

Once there, I expected to see a river full of interesting birds, but I saw only Mallards and the commonest gulls.

Wind gusts of 40 mph or more made it feel colder than mid-50s temperatures would have suggested, and very light intermittent rain fell.

It felt even chillier on the unsheltered 70th Street Pier, where I encountered Jacob Drucker pivoting his scope in search of birds. He mentioned that after his initial sightings this morning he had not seen anything else of interest.

Jacob had fallen out of contention on the "Top Birders" leader board, a result only of his being away at college in Massachusetts. I was glad that for the rest of the year he and I would not be in competition; I have no idea if he cared about the rankings, but it made me feel more comfortable about sharing sightings and strategies.

After ten minutes I was already getting chilled and still not seeing any scoters, so I wandered back to the relative shelter of the Greenway.

I needed to pee, but as I walked along the usual options appeared to be closed, including the public Greenway facilities and even those of the Boat Basin Café. I had often used a porta-potty at the 93rd Street Playground in Riverside Park, so I walked another half-mile to it, but the porta-potty was not there, and regular restrooms were locked.

I would have to find a restaurant or diner with restrooms, and this meant walking to Broadway and then searching. Many places were closed. I found one that was open, bought a bagel, and availed myself of the facilities.

Now, after nearly an hour delay, I was ready to return to the Hudson and continue the watch. I felt that I was already falling behind. In addition to missing the scoters, I had also missed the Royal Tern that was reported early from the Inwood Hill area. On the bright side, no new reports of rarities had come in since I left the Greenway.

Conditions appeared the same—still no good birds on the river. There was, however, a disturbing new development: police were now moving up and down the Greenway with loudspeakers, telling people that the park was closed and that they should leave. Response to these warnings was tepid; mostly, people just kept moving along to other points on the Greenway.

After 45 minutes I had had enough. The police did not want us here; the weather was cold and wet; and the desired birds were not showing up. Discouraged with the whole idea of hurricane birding, I exited the park and caught a bus back to the East Side.

Just before 1 p.m. I saw an online posting from Andrew Farnsworth, who had made a late-morning trip to Randall's Island. He had Black Scoters, Bonaparte's Gulls, and a single Royal Tern. He had finally come back to tie me at 189 birds.

He had driven there in his car. Driving was not an option for me, and I was not about to try running across the RFK Bridge or the 103rd Street pedestrian bridge during a storm. Officials were warning that high winds could force bridges to be closed at any time. I did not want to get stranded on Randall's Island in my running clothes with a hurricane on the way.

For my afternoon birding I decided to try the East River, which was just a fifteen-minute stroll from my apartment. At 83rd Street I found a walkway with a roof overhead and buildings blocking winds on the west.

I needed this protection, because by then the winds had really picked up, with gusts of 90 mph, and the rain had become heavier. *This* was a hurricane, and plenty of other people wanted to run or walk along the shore while it raged on, enjoying a rare display of nature's power from a safe, elevated location. I watched gulls beating their wings furiously, trying to fly north against the wind. Amazingly, most of them succeeded, though at times they appeared to make no progress or were driven even further back.

I ended up with two good sightings, a Bonaparte's Gull (not new) and bird number 190, a female Black Scoter. I could take the big year lead to bed with me for one more night.

The rain and wind intensified as evening fell, with Sandy's eye passing through Atlantic City, New Jersey, 110 miles south of Manhattan. From there, Sandy weakened and drifted west, but not before causing massive damage.

Sandy devastated the New York coastline, mainly through flooding (its nearest approach to New York City coincided with high tide) and caused widespread power outages in New York and New Jersey areas served by overhead wires, as wind gusts of over 100 mph brought down trees. Over 30,000 people lost their homes. Millions along the East Coast were left without electric power, and many would wait nearly two weeks to have it restored. Residents of lower Manhattan were without power or subway service for five days. Nearly all those living north of 39th Street in Manhattan maintained their electric power, and I felt fortunate to be among them.

I awoke early on October 30 around 6:45 a.m. and planned to meet with Farnsworth for birding on the Hudson. Having endured the previous day's birding debacle, I knew what to expect and prepared accordingly. All public restrooms would again be closed, so I had no extra liquids with my breakfast. I did not like being dehydrated, but I knew it was the only way I was going to be able to bird the entire morning without having to take a break and risk missing a rare sighting.

As I ran through Central Park and the Upper West Side on 86th Street I could see numerous fallen trees and several cars that had been crushed by them.

I wanted to begin birding at the 79th Street Boat Basin, an indoor café with an open view of the adjacent Hudson River, but the paved path to it was again blocked by a web of police tape. I could go under the tape, but what if I encountered police? There was no way I could claim to have not seen the tape. Just as I had done yesterday, I ran further south and found a path to the Greenway where a single strand of tape had been pushed down.

I reached the river at 8:25 a.m. and walked toward the 70th Street Pier. I immediately noticed large numbers of Forster's Terns moving north over the river. This was a new species for me, one that I had tried to get many times during the summer without success. Other than this, I was not seeing anything else new or interesting.

Within a half-hour, another problem arose: police were clearing people off the pier and off the Greenway, this time more aggressively than the day before. Soon the pier was empty, and those on the Greenway were being directed to make their exits now. Sometime after 9 a.m. I exited the Greenway near 67th Street.

I did not want to stop birding, and I found that the Riverside Drive area around 67th Street afforded the closest legal view of the river but not really a very good one. Instead of being right on the shore, I was 220 yards away. At that distance I could still identify a duck even farther out, but I would have almost no chance with a smaller storm-petrel.

Those observing with scopes from the Boat Basin saw exactly that, a Leach's Storm-Petrel, just after 9 a.m. before it was attacked and killed by gulls. These observers must have entered the café from off the Greenway. The chase pack of birders in third place and below had gained a bird on me yesterday by observing two species of scoter to my one. Now they were gaining one more bird.

At 9:45 a.m. I texted Farnsworth to find out what he was doing. He wrote back that he had been on the 70th Street Pier and then walked north after it was cleared. I told him where I was, and he said he was now walking my way and would see me shortly. Fifteen minutes later I had still not heard from him, so I checked in again and learned that he had actually gone to the Boat Basin, which was providing good views. He suggested that I do the same.

I did not like the idea of sneaking into a location that that the police clearly indicated was off limits, but if Farnsworth was there I figured it must be OK. I went around the tape and at 10:30 a.m. entered the café to find a dozen of the area's top birders scanning the river with their binoculars and scopes.

This was the first time Farnsworth and I had met in person. He was actively surveying the full viewing area, south, north, low and high, and calling out birds as he saw them.

Earlier that morning, off the Pier, he had observed American Wigeon (a migrating duck) and American Oystercatcher (a large, red-billed shorebird seen frequently at the Jamaica Bay refuge in Queens but almost never in Manhattan; it would fall under the "displaced coastal species" category and had also appeared on the Hudson during Irene). This meant he had now re-taken the lead for the first time since January.

I was glad that I had joined him, as any birds observed by him or any of the other birders at the Basin would be shared. With the collective talent and optical power here, I was much better off than on my own.

We observed nearly a hundred Forster's Terns moving by, along with a much smaller number of Bonaparte's Gulls. We also saw such common birds as American Coot, Common Loon, Red-throated Loon, and Red-breasted Merganser.

At 11 a.m. Farnsworth pointed out a Black Skimmer flying low, up the river, to the north. Since this was a species he had already counted but that I needed, I much appreciated his help in getting it. Along with the Forster's Tern, it had been one of my "white whale" birds of the summer.

Later, Farnsworth would find an even better bird. He got everyone focused on three dark, gull-like birds high over the Hudson—Jaegers, all of them, but were they Pomarine or Parasitic? One member of the group kept asking Farnsworth where the Jaegers were, and Farnsworth patiently offered help and directed viewers to them with his free arm. Viewing conditions were poor—overcast and hazy with light rain falling.

Regrettably the time he spent providing directions, along with the bad conditions, likely prevented him from getting better views during the Jaegers' closest approaches and Farnsworth was unable to say for sure whether we had seen Pomarine or Parasitic, though he strongly suspected one of the former and two of the latter. Therefore we could not add these to our species totals. A reliable birder along the Chelsea waterfront reported one Pomarine and two Parasitic Jaegers shortly after our sighting, lending credence to Farnsworth's suspicions.

Farnsworth had to leave after noon, but he was not done birding, and he was about to get the most improbable observation of the day. At 12:30 p.m., at 54ᵗʰ and Sixth Avenue, right in the middle of midtown Manhattan, he noticed a "nighthawk-like bird attempting to evade a Peregrine Falcon." He was able to observe it for two minutes and got good views—a Leach's Storm-Petrel!

By 1:18 p.m. Farnsworth was at 51ˢᵗ Street and the East River, his customary viewing grounds, where he saw a weary juvenile Northern Gannet being attacked in the water by Great Black-backed Gulls. This was the first report of Northern Gannet in Manhattan during Sandy, and it put Farnsworth solidly in the lead in our competition.

I had left the Boat Basin at 1:45 when a park ranger told everyone that they had to exit. The Greenway had already been cleared, and we had been hiding every time the police passed by. We knew our stay there was over and that we would not be able to return. This was fine, as we were not seeing any new birds, and after more than five hours of birding I wanted to drink water and have lunch.

Farnsworth, however, was *still* not done. After lunch he returned to the East River shore and at 3:30 he spotted five Pomarine Jaegers flying south. He had completed a *tour de force* of hurricane birding!

I visited the East River myself soon after his last observation but was not able to see anything interesting.

I ended the day having lost the big year lead but having gained even greater respect both for Farnsworth's birding skills and for his interest in helping other birders. His generosity was obvious during our encounter with the jaegers on the Hudson and it continued throughout the rest of the day. Farnsworth sent out text alerts quickly and often, so that others could have a chance to observe the rarities he was finding. He offered helpful advice whenever I emailed or texted him. He was by all appearances a decent guy, well-liked and well-respected by the other top birders.

Still, I wanted to regain my lead.

After getting some extra sleep, I and considered where to bird on Wednesday, October 31. Yesterday's closure meant no going back to the Hudson Greenway. All the city parks, including Central Park, were still closed. We will never know what interesting birds Central Park held during the time it was closed, but I suspect it had some excellent fallout waterfowl on the Reservoir and the Lake. Randall's Island seemed to be the clear choice for birding, as the bridges to it were open and it was a multi-purpose area, not just a park, so it would likely remain accessible.

The problem was that subways were not yet operating, so I could not take the Lexington Avenue line to 125th Street and then run across the RFK Bridge to the northern shoreline as I usually did. Instead I would have to enter the island by running to and across the 103rd Street pedestrian bridge.

Once there, I continued running a paved path north along the East River toward the restored salt-marsh. Just where the path turned east and the salt-marsh began, I hit a roadblock, literally—a metal barrier with the dreaded yellow police tape around it completely blocking the narrow path.

Could I have gone over or around it? Certainly, but there was no way I could deny having encountered it if a police officer approached me, and I was not going to risk a trespassing arrest for an uncertain chance to see birds. I ran back home.

At 2:15 p.m. I received an alert of a Golden Eagle flyover viewed from Harlem and now believed to be near 86th and Fifth Avenue, just blocks away. I ran outside and west toward Fifth. The area just north of the Metropolitan Museum afforded the widest view, but I never saw the eagle. I had done many hours of dedicated raptor-watching this fall with the hope of again seeing a Golden Eagle, as I had the previous October, but had not seen any.

Late in the afternoon I received an eBird report of a Vesper Sparrow observed just northwest of the restored saltmarsh on Randall's Island by Ben Cacace. I immediately wrote to him and asked how he had been able to reach it. He said that workers had created an opening next to the barricade after removing some downed trees. It seems that I had arrived a couple hours too early.

I had not gotten any new birds on the 31st, but neither had any of the other leaders. Farnsworth had 194; I had 192; and Anders Peltomaa, who had gotten all the birds seen at the Boat Basin on the 30th, including an early Dunlin fly-by, had rallied to 179.

Had I chosen to pass under the yellow tape, I would have had those birds, too. Instead, I had spent much of the morning standing hundreds of yards offshore, seeing nothing.

This is just the sort of thing I feared might go wrong with hurricane birding: small choices resulting in vastly different outcomes and no opportunity to improve them. The Leach's Storm-Petrel that the Boat Basin group saw on the 30th was quickly killed, and dead birds cannot be counted (not that there would have been anything left to see.). The Dunlin and the White-winged Scoters continued northward and were not seen again.

Sandy's late-season arrival prevented it from bringing more birds, as many coastal species had already migrated further south. This was good for me, as it limited the opportunities for others to catch up. I was also fortunate that Sandy's eye passed so far south of New York, because it meant that Manhattan did not get any entrained species, just displaced ones.

Hurricane Irene had been a summer storm whose eye passed almost directly over New York City, and it turned out to be far more productive for birders while causing much less damage to the city, bringing many species, including tropical ones like Sooty and Bridled Tern, and White-tailed Tropicbird, and allowing Farnsworth to increase his species total for 2011 by roughly fifteen birds. Farnsworth did as well as anyone with Sandy and added only eight birds.

On Thursday, November 1, limited subway service was restored to uptown trains, so I went for a 9 a.m. visit to Randall's Island. First I explored the north shore for unusual waterfowl but did not see any. Then I went south to the area just east of the Icahn Stadium parking lot where Cacace yesterday had reported the Vesper Sparrow, which he said had been associating with a lone Dark-eyed Junco. I quickly found the junco, but an hour of wandering, watching, and waiting did not produce the Vesper Sparrow. I ran back home.

At 12:05, shortly after I had begun eating lunch, one of the odder bird reports appeared online: a reputable birder had received a photo from a friend of an American Woodcock *walking* along 52nd Street near Fifth Avenue. This was just the sort of alert for which I had been waiting ever since Farnsworth had heard his American Woodcocks calling during a nighttime flyover. I got on the subway and was on the scene in 20 minutes. I searched 52nd and surrounding streets but did not find the bird.

The big news of the early morning had been the Northern Gannets seen in New York Harbor. Since the subway was not moving past 42nd Street, I had no practical way to chase them.

Great news, however, arrived in a 12:50 p.m. text alert: Northern Gannet were being observed southwest of the 70th Street Pier (which apparently had been reopened) on the Hudson. I briefly considered going directly there from 52nd and Fifth, but after the long run and failed woodcock chase I really needed to sit down and have lunch.

I took the subway back home and emailed Farnsworth about my morning. Then, rested and recharged, I took the cross-town bus to 79th and Broadway and ran the rest of the way to the pier.

The Northern Gannet were magnificent! They were larger

than even Great Black-backed Gulls, with long, slim, black-tipped wings and long, capacious bills for scooping up fish. Their method of hunting was distinctive: they would soar high and then rapidly plunge-dive at their underwater targets.

I should have stopped then and returned home, but I decided to proceed back to midtown for another chance at the American Woodcock. This required another two miles of walking/running and plenty of retraced steps as I moved east and west along the streets.

I never saw the woodcock, and a message posted to the boards later explained why. It seems that early in the afternoon the bird had landed on top of a midtown firehouse, and a firefighter found it unwilling to fly and took it under his care for delivery to a wildlife expert.

The Northern Gannet ended up being the best of my four hurricane birds and perhaps the only real one, in the sense that the other three occurred infrequently in Manhattan anyway—though not often in late October. The gannets would linger on the Hudson for another two days.

I had 193 birds to Farnsworth's 194. It had been a terrible week for me, but the big year contest was far from over.

37

POST-SANDY RESURGENCE

I knew that if I continued to bird intelligently and actively, as I had throughout the year, my good fortune would eventually return. I just did not know when.

I was looking forward to the Saturday, November 3, partial reopening of Central Park. With my girlfriend unable to make it into the city, I would have all day to bird. Clear skies and strong northwest winds boded well.

My main goal was to get the Eastern Bluebird. It was time for this species to be passing through. I had had one in late October last year, and Farnsworth had observed some (again) the previous day in a midtown flyover. It was a difficult bird to get in Central Park, generally presenting in low numbers and during a tight migration window.

I figured that the Great Hill area would be excellent both for it and for a number of other species, including perhaps the Vesper Sparrow, and I began heading there at 8:45 a.m.

Along the way I had several Red-shouldered Hawks, not a new species but one I enjoyed seeing and one that was indicative of continued good raptor migration.

Shortly after arriving on the Great Hill, I saw a bright blue bird perching on a branch just south of the Children's Glade—an

Eastern Bluebird! My big year luck was back. Last year I recall searching for days to find one. This year it took all of half an hour.

After 90 minutes of raptor-watching and sparrow-hunting on the Great Hill, I decided to head over to Riverside Park on the Hudson, which offered the best odds (so I thought) for a Golden Eagle.

During thirty minutes there I had a half-dozen each of migrating Red-tailed Hawks and Turkey Vultures but no new birds. So I started walking east, back toward Central Park.

By the time I arrived at Central Park West I had been birding for nearly five hours and I considered going directly home, but I figured it would not take that much longer to go a bit further south and wind my way through the Ramble.

I walked up to Belvedere Castle, where someone was using a scope to raptor-watch, and then down into the Ramble proper. As I was passing by on my way to the Oven, I noticed a collection of birders at the southeast corner of Evodia Field looking intently almost straight up. This demanded investigating!

As I arrived and began scanning the tree, one of them said there was an owl up there. I saw it right away and exclaimed, "That is a Barred Owl!"

Now my luck really had turned. I had picked up two birds today, one good (Eastern Bluebird) and the other great (the owl). I had finally atoned for missing the Barred Owl in January. I felt mentally sharp again and confident. I should have moved back into the big year lead. But I hadn't.

Farnsworth had been birding Peter Detmold Park in Sutton Place since 7:20 a.m. and had already issued numerous text alerts about what he was seeing. He had noted the excellent raptor flight, including Red-shouldered, Sharp-shinned, and Red-tailed Hawks, along with Turkey Vultures.

He also had alerted everyone to a strong flight of American Pipits, a species not previously observed in Manhattan for the year. Pipits are gray-brown, sparrow-like birds with pale eye-stripes. Their name derives from their high *"pip-it"* calls. They are, in general common birds, and they pass over Manhattan regularly in fall migration. Nevertheless, they are reported in Central Park very rarely, perhaps once per year, and then only by a few of the top birders. It seems that they simply do not touch down much over Manhattan, which is odd because their preferred habitat is grassy, open fields and Central Park has these in abundance. The previous sentence could also describe Bobolink, a less common bird also best observed in flyovers, or Eastern Meadowlark.

In fact, Farnsworth also announced a single flyover Eastern Meadowlark, a bird I had been working hard to get on land without success. A few put in a brief appearance on the Central Park Great Lawn last year. Previously, I wanted to get it so I could pull ahead; now I needed it just to keep pace.

Farnsworth is the undisputed champion of flyover birding. He is one of the world's top authorities on flight calls, and he is superbly skilled at visually identifying birds in flight, even when they are flying high. He gets a very large percentage of his sightings as flyovers, for which his apartment—a high-rise overlooking the East River, right on a popular migration pathway—is ideally suited. Many birds that are never seen on land in Manhattan occasionally pass overhead—for example, Short-eared Owl, for which Farnsworth has the only Manhattan eBird reports on record.

I could not identify many passerines in flyover with the level of certainty required to claim them on an eBird report, so I sought them out in places where they were most likely to land. The large, open fields of the North End, along with the even more expansive and little-used fields of Randall's Island seemed like the best places to find birds such as Bobolink, Eastern Meadowlark, and American Pipit. The first had already passed through weeks ago, but I still had a shot at the last two.

In fact, I would learn in the evening that a reliable birder had observed an Eastern Meadowlark and possibly another Vesper Sparrow on one of the northern baseball fields of Randall's Island. I would make it my first stop the next morning.

Another flyover species Farnsworth added on November 3 was even better: Evening Grosbeak, which had not been reported in Central Park since 1998. I actually was glad to learn that Farnsworth had seen five of these birds flying west at 9:30 a.m. because I had been anticipating their arrival in Manhattan after recent reports in nearby New Jersey and I was looking forward to seeing them. Evening Grosbeak are large, colorful finches with massive bills. I assumed that everyone would soon have them, and it was fine that Farnsworth got them first.

Soon I learned that Farnsworth's day was even better than I had thought. He had observed two unusual ducks, American Wigeon and Northern Pintail, with the latter being a new bird for the year. I had wigeon last year on Turtle Pond; it was rare for Manhattan but common enough in the general area that I thought I would eventually see it, perhaps at Randall's Island or maybe on the Reservoir. Northern Pintail, in contrast, had not been reported on eBird in Central Park since 2007; there was little hope of getting it.

Now Farnsworth held a three-bird lead over me.

I began Sunday the Fourth with a very early (7:45 a.m.) visit to the northern shore of Randall's Island, but I was unable to see the meadowlark or any rare sparrows despite over three hours of birding. I ran back across the RFK Bridge and took the subway home.

At 12:10 p.m. I received a text alert of two Evening Grosbeaks in the trees of the blowdown meadow on the southeast edge of the Great Hill. I ran over and was the first birder on the scene. The original finder, Sam Stuart, had a camera out and was taking pictures of the loudly-chirping female birds. It was a historic moment for Central Park birding: the return of the Evening Grosbeaks after a 14-year absence. I took plenty of time to enjoy observing them as they fed on the fruiting trees. As I was leaving Storm Field I encountered a large group containing some of the area's most dedicated birders, who had walked from the Ramble to see the grosbeaks. I told them the birds were still being seen, and I headed toward the southern slope of the Great Hill to look for other species.

While I was looking for raptors and sparrows, a woman who regularly birds the park approached me to ask where the grosbeaks were. I gave her directions, and as she was leaving she asked if I had seen the owl in Shakespeare Garden. She said that there had been a Northern Saw-whet Owl there earlier, low in a pine tree near the entrance from the Belvedere Castle area. I thanked her for the tip and headed directly for the 103rd Street stop on the C line, just a block away.

In twenty minutes I was at the overlook to Shakespeare Garden where I saw several people peering into one of the trees. I joined them and was amazed to see a small owl, clearly a Northern Saw-whet, roosting in a yew tree, well-hidden but only eight feet off the ground and just a couple feet in from the outer edge of the tree. I took a quick, diagnostic view and then left, not wanting to stress the owl. I later learned online that a park ranger soon came by and placed a barrier to protect the owl from overzealous viewers.

I was relieved to have observed the owl, probably the very same one that I had been prevented from seeing by the early closing of Central Park on October 28. In two days I had made up nearly my entire owl deficit for the year. I had also added two other birds, Eastern Bluebird and Evening Grosbeak.

With a fifteen-bird lead over my next-nearest competitor and migration season coming to a close, I was putting second place out of reach for everyone else. The race for the title would be between Farnsworth and me.

Meanwhile, Farnsworth was busy putting first place further out of *my* reach, birding nonstop from Peter Detmold Park beginning at 7:55 a.m. and later from his apartment until after 4:30 p.m.

He was again sending out text alerts of his sightings and general observations of another very strong migration day. He was relentless!

His first new bird of the day was Horned Lark, seen flying over the East River. This species was almost never observed in Manhattan—the only historical eBird records of it were from Farnsworth and all were as flyovers. I figured that I had little chance of ever seeing this bird.

Like the American Pipit, the Horned Lark is generally a common bird, seen in flocks on grass and open ground (it prefers the latter) in the eastern United States but more frequently in the Midwest. The lush grass fields of Central and other Manhattan parks may not be to its liking; it is a mega-rarity there and throughout most of New York City. Many sightings do, however, come from Floyd Bennett Field in southern Brooklyn.

Farnsworth's second new bird of the day took the wind right out of me: Golden Eagle. I was already at home by the time he started observing it and texting about it at 2:50 p.m.

I had been searching the skies for Golden Eagles on most clear days with the right winds for weeks. I had been following various mountain-based hawk watches further upstate in New York, and had read that this was an excellent year for Golden Eagles. I had seen one the previous year in late October, and mine was one of only two prior eBird observations of the species in Manhattan. I was doing everything possible to see one again.

Had I been in Central Park at the right time, I might have seen this one, as Farnsworth said that this is where the bird was when he initially viewed it. He saw it, over a mile away, from Sutton Place with a scope. In his later observations, where he confirmed that it was indeed a juvenile Golden Eagle because of the characteristic white patches at the base of its primaries and tail, the bird may have been two miles away over the Hudson River. I could only marvel at his combination of visual acuity and optical resolving power.

I had a lot of work to do. Farnsworth had added many great birds over the weekend, but I still had time to get most of them.

I set out at 9 a.m. on Monday, doing an early raptor watch on the Great Lawn by Turtle Pond. I saw a Peregrine Falcon and a Turkey Vulture but nothing new.

Meanwhile, Farnsworth had sent out an early report of White-winged Crossbills, another of the irruptive finches, which was a new species for him (and for everyone) for the year. He noted that the two birds he saw were flying west toward Central Park. Farnsworth's ability to get everything first was becoming more than a little dispiriting.

I went out again to the Great Lawn after lunch. There was a seemingly endless progression of Red-tailed Hawks flying over, close to 20 in little more than an hour. I also had a great sighting for Central Park, for which I sent out an alert: an immature Bald Eagle. Still, I saw nothing new.

I returned home just before 3 p.m., but was soon roused back into action by a 3:22 p.m. text alert. White-winged Crossbills were being seen on the overlook to Shakespeare Garden, right where the Red Crossbills had appeared first in August.

I already had running clothes on, and I was on the scene in ten minutes. Many of the park's regular birders were already there. I saw the crossbills immediately, both male and female, low in the surrounding hemlock trees, and I could hear their loud trills.

The species was a very rare visitor to Central Park. The only other eBird record of it there, or anywhere in Manhattan, was from 2009. This small flock of roughly five birds remained in the Shakespeare Garden area for another two days and then moved on. More were seen in the park in mid- and late December.

I did not stick around long to watch the crossbills. I do not enjoy crowds of birders, and I had another bird on my mind: the American Tree Sparrow, my longtime nemesis. A birder had seen one in the morning just west of the tennis courts and reported it online later in the afternoon. The location was nearby and worth a shot.

I found a small flock of Dark-eyed Juncos with which the tree sparrow must have been associating. Mixed in was at least one Chipping Sparrow. But I could not find the sparrow I wanted.

After my failure to re-find the American Tree Sparrow that Lenore Swenson saw on October 23, the bird had become my new white whale. I would return to search the area west of the tennis courts several times again beginning the next day, but I never did end up seeing this particular bird.

With the birds of the weekend and November 5 counted, the eBird scoreboard read Farnsworth 201, Barrett 198.

38

BARNACLE GOOSE

Much of my birding involves quickly "chasing" reports of rarities and reaching them before they are gone. If you want to have a successful big year, you need to be able to chase—it is the most efficient way to observe the rarest species. Of course I also go birding to observe whatever is out there, even when there are no active alerts. When doing so, I still try to think about what new species I could possibly encounter, and I bird in a way that increases my chances of observing them.

"Finders" or "spotters" enjoy the latter sort of birding. They are patient and perceptive. They enjoy being out in the park and seeing whatever they can; they are also willing to spend many fruitless hours searching in order to be the original finder of a rarity. I very much appreciate what they do.

In this chapter I get to be both the chaser *and* the finder of a historically-significant rare bird.

On Sunday, November 11, in the late afternoon, I received a "Year Needs" email from eBird. This list came from an experienced, reliable birder who birded the Inwood area in northern Manhattan and reported a Barnacle Goose, which she described as a "Black, white and gray goose, about the size of a Brant. Black head, neck, and breast with a white face and a small black bill. Gray back with dark bars. White belly and flanks." This description fit Barnacle Goose perfectly.

Barnacle Geese breed in Arctic regions of the North Atlantic and winter in the Scottish Isles and Eurasia. Each fall, some make the mistake of following the west coast of the Atlantic south rather than the east coast and end up in North America. They have become rare but regular vagrants to the northeastern United States.

Barnacle Geese are also popular with waterfowl collectors—they are good-looking birds and are easy to keep. Some Barnacle Geese observed in the wild are found, from their banding, to be escaped (or possibly released) birds. One has to be careful to look for evidence of prior ownership, particularly when a Barnacle Goose is observed at a time of year inconsistent with a migration error.

Among New York State birders a Barnacle Goose is big news, worthy of an immediate alert, as many birders will want to see it. For example, on October 24 a Barnacle Goose was found in Prospect Park in Brooklyn. This bird attracted a great deal of attention and lingered for three days.

It therefore puzzled me that the original finder of the Barnacle Goose in Inwood did not do anything to notify other birders of her rare find. She had finished birding by 1:45 p.m. and did not even enter her list into eBird until hours later in the day.

There was also another problem: she gave no explicit location for the bird.

I had no way of contacting the finder to learn more, but I knew someone who could: Andrew Farnsworth, who is in charge of reviewing eBird data submitted in New York County. I suggested that he get in touch with the finder through the standard eBird review process—meaning, send her an email asking for more details.

He wrote back that he had just done so, but I did not hear from him again during the evening. Before I went to bed, I emailed Farnsworth again to let him know that I planned to go to Inwood early the next morning even if he did not get the location info.

I had done some thinking, and, with much of Inwood Hill Park and all of Swindler Cove Park closed for storm damage repair, I had narrowed down the possible sighting locations to two places: 1) the Dyckman Street ball fields and the picnic area just north of them, which always attract plenty of geese; or 2) the saltmarsh bay on the east side of Inwood Hill Park and the ball fields south of it.

When I awoke the next morning, I still had not heard more from Farnsworth, so I planned to check the Inwood places in the above order.

I arrived at the Dyckman Street ball fields at 9:15 a.m. A thick fog hung over the park and the nearby Hudson River. Visibility was roughly 100 yards. As I walked further across the fields I observed a decent number of common birds—White-throated and Song Sparrows, Dark-eyed Juncos, chickadees, titmice, and even a Northern Mockingbird. I finally saw a dozen Canada Geese near the compost heap. I examined each one carefully, afraid of overlooking the Barnacle Goose, but all of them were indeed Canadas. I scanned the edges of the field but I did not see any other geese.

I texted Farnsworth that I was moving on to the east side of the park, where I arrived after retracing my steps and then walking another fifteen minutes along adjacent streets.

There I saw a hundred Canada Geese milling about on the more distant baseball field. Among them was a single Barnacle Goose. I was ecstatic! I looked it over carefully, not wanting draw the entire local birding community here over a false ID, but there was no mistaking it. I could not see any banding on it, so I had to assume it was a wild bird.

I texted Farnsworth, who helped me by issuing a text alert. Anders Peltomaa relayed the text alert online. Farnsworth said he was on the way here, and I figured that within forty minutes I would be joined by a collection of birders. I called Starr Saphir, who lived just a short walk from there. She was thrilled and said that she would be on the way. She also told me that she could recall no prior occurrence of Barnacle Goose in Manhattan, and she had been following birding news since the 1940s.

Farnsworth ended up being delayed by a flat tire, but after a little over an hour he still was the first to arrive on the scene. He confirmed the ID and began taking photographs. Anders arrived shortly thereafter, also with a camera.

I soon saw Starr walking slowly on the far side of the baseball field. I called her cell, and she told me she was seeing the bird and that she was not going to come all the way over to the other side, as her friend needed to head off to the airport. This was the last time I ever saw her.

Farnsworth was watching for other birds, too, and he pointed out an extremely rare one, a single Black Vulture flying with a single Turkey Vulture. I had already seen Black Vulture earlier in the year, as had he, and aside from our observations there was only one other record of the species in Manhattan during the entire year.

I mentioned to Farnsworth what Starr told me, and he agreed that this probably was the first recorded occurrence of Barnacle Goose in Manhattan.

By 12:25 p.m. Anders had to return to his classes, and Farnsworth suggested we bird the nearby saltmarsh area, so I joined him. We saw good birds—Peregrines, a Merlin hunting over the Inwood Hill forest, and a Great Blue Heron standing on the saltmarsh shore.

We would soon do even better. As we were just about to finish the walk, Farnsworth heard and saw a flock of 30 American Pipits flying almost directly overhead and west toward Inwood Hill. I caught a glimpse of them as they flew away. I am not sure I would have noticed these had he not alerted me. He, as you may recall, had previously listed the species, so he allowed me to gain a bird on him and cut my deficit to two. It was also my 200th species of the year, a milestone that I had not suspected I would reach even after a strong spring season. I had many reasons to celebrate a memorable day at Inwood Hill Park.

39

LESSER BLACK-BACKED GULL

Two days later, on the morning of November 14, I was thinking about heading up to Inwood again. Horned Lark had been observed at Van Cortlandt Park just to the north in the Bronx, and it was likely that they would also pass through Inwood Hill. Farnsworth had mentioned that vagrant Cave Swallows seemed possible there, too. It was also the best spot to see a Golden Eagle.

I was dressed and ready to go when an 8:56 a.m. text alert arrived from Farnsworth. He had reported a Lesser Black-backed Gull across the Bronx Kill, visible from the northeast shore of Randall's Island. He also had observed a flyover of more American Pipits.

I took the subway to 125th Street and then rode the bus across the RFK Bridge to the northeast ball fields, arriving at 9:30 a.m. The gulls appeared to have moved from the New York Post building to an adjacent one, but they were still lined up on the closest ledge. This is when I really could have used a scope or stronger binoculars, as I was near the limit of my optics.

Soon I saw what had to be the adult Lesser Black-backed Gull. It had a yellow bill and yellow legs, dark gray (not black) wings, and streaking along the back of its head and neck. It even flew out later over the Randall's Island shore, allowing me to observe it in Manhattan territory.

Lesser Black-backed Gulls are uncommon but regular visitors to the East Coast from Europe. They have only a few historical eBird records in Manhattan, though they have many on the southern shore of Long Island. I suspect they would be recorded more in Manhattan if birders looked for them more actively; searching through hundreds of similar-looking gulls for one with subtle differences is not something most birders want to do. I know I don't.

I looked around the north shore for pipits and Vesper Sparrows, but I was not seeing any and decided to continue south over the rest of the island, which might still offer the species I sought.

After rounding the bend past the restored saltmarsh, I followed the dirt path past a median strip with flower and shrub plantings. A large sparrow on the ground nearby caught my eye. I slowly raised my binoculars so as not to frighten it. I immediately noticed its red crown and dark central breast spot—it was an American Tree Sparrow! I had finally found my white whale. I wanted to enjoy some minutes viewing it and its bicolored bill after all the hours I had spent trying to find it in the North End and by the tennis courts.

After walking across the 103rd Street pedestrian bridge, I continued on foot to nearby Conservatory Garden in Central Park where a likely Rufous Hummingbird had been found the previous day. I wanted to observe it, even though I had already seen the species on the first day of the year, because this one could possibly turn out to be a different member of the genus *Selasphorus*, such as an Allen's Hummingbird. High-speed photos of the tail-spread would be required to tell the difference. These were soon posted online, and the bird turned out to be just another Rufous Hummingbird as I suspected.

I was now only one bird off the big year lead: 202 to Farnsworth's 203. I did not know it then, but despite the recent flurry of new birds I was about to enter an extended birding drought that would go on nearly a month before it ended.

40

NO BIRDS FOR YOU!

Throughout much of the fall, Yellow-rumped Warblers are almost annoyingly abundant. They are seen in the trees and often on the ground (along with Palm Warblers), and as a birder you need to look at them to be sure that they are not some other more interesting bird.

By late October their numbers have already fallen, but you continue to see a few of them each day even into early November, tiny reminders of the great fall migration that is at its end.

By mid-November even these few have disappeared, and the park starts to seem more barren and cold. You can still raptor-watch, but most hawks have already passed through and the slim chance of seeing a Golden Eagle is getting slimmer each day.

I had my targets, and among them was the Snow Goose. It is an understatement to say that the Snow Goose is abundant. Unlike many species which have been in sharp decline since the 1970s, the Snow Goose has increased its population in North America perhaps several times over. Biologists are rightly concerned that there may too many of these geese, and hunting regulators have responded with longer seasons and generous daily bag limits.

You would think, then, that seeing just a single Snow Goose in Manhattan would be easy. The area is right on a coastal flyway. You can see hundreds of Canada Geese every day. Yet Snow Geese remain elusive here.

Farnsworth would be the only Manhattan birder to record Snow Goose on eBird in 2012, and even he had only a few sightings in small numbers. It appears from the records that Snow Geese, which were observed frequently in upstate New York and often in large flocks, mostly chose to fly either east of Manhattan, over Brooklyn and Long Island, or west of Manhattan, over eastern New Jersey.

Another target was Green-winged Teal. Every year at least one visits the Reservoir. I began running laps around it, binoculars in hand, as I had done for the Common Loon in 2011. Had I simply gone out to the Lake on October 28, I would have seen a pair of them, as did an entire birding group that day.

No one else saw any of the birds I needed until November 20, when Matthew Rymkiewicz issued a text alert at 8 a.m. of a Common Redpoll in the trees above the western end of the Gill in the Ramble.

Common Redpoll was the last of the irruptive finches expected to appear in Central Park. I had been following the progress of the species south into Westchester County and knew that it was only a matter of time before it showed up in Manhattan.

I did not go out to the Ramble for well over an hour—I was sleeping later now that early morning birding was no longer necessary, but my delay was not to blame for what would turn out to be a failed chase. The big mistake I made was in assuming that the Common Redpoll would move through the Ramble quickly, likely as part of a flock, and that I needed to look elsewhere for it. Since the species prefers birch catkins, I searched my tree map for white birch. The shore of the Lake just southwest of Bow Bridge has them. I also figured that Common Redpoll might like the dawn redwoods atop Strawberry Fields, whose cones had initially attracted the Pine Siskins.

Though I did look where the Common Redpoll was reported, I did not search the trees there thoroughly enough before moving on. If I had, I probably would have seen the bird. Other birders reported the Redpoll again in those trees at 11:30 a.m. The species was not observed again in the following days.

On the next day, November 21, a quiet afternoon was interrupted by an eBird "Year Needs" email at 2:05 p.m. Jacob Drucker had observed Black-headed Gull and Horned Lark on northeast Randall's Island near where the Nelson's Sparrows had been. I needed both. He wrote that the Black-headed Gull had flown away toward into the Bronx. I thought the Horned Lark might still be hanging around.

I was on location by 3 p.m., but I was not able re-find these birds, and I did not see anything else of interest. My success rate at chasing was plummeting!

I did have an exciting find while running in the Ramble two days later, on the morning of November 23. I noticed a single birder looking intently at a tree near Azalea Pond. Soon several birders had assembled there and one of them was a local hawk photographer who specialized in covering Pale Male. I stopped beside them, followed their focus into the tree, and was treated to a handsome Great Horned Owl perched on a branch.

I had seen this owl species twice before during the year, but it is a majestic bird that is always thrilling to see. It was also high enough in the tree and protected from viewers by off-trail brush so that viewing the owl would not unduly stress it. I reported it on eBird with a clear, specific location so that other birders could enjoy it, too.

That day was special—a "Three Owl Day in Central Park," as I wrote on my blog. In addition to the Great Horned Owl, which remained in the Ramble for a nearly a week, two other owl species (Barred and Northern Saw-whet) were continuing in the park.

The Barred Owl that I saw on November 3 stayed only for a day. On November 12, however, three Barred Owls were seen in the area west of the Great Lawn. These owls lingered well into December, and at least one was present through year-end and into April 2013.

Indeed, late fall 2012 had brought an irruption of Barred Owls across much of the East Coast, including Connecticut and Massachusetts, where a number of them were observed right in the middle of the city on Boston Common.

A Northern Saw-whet Owl, probably the same one from November 4, was seen again in Shakespeare Garden on November 19 and in days following.

I believed that my best hope for a new species was some sort of duck. I could see that a couple of good ducks, namely Green-winged Teal and American Wigeon, were being observed in areas adjacent to Manhattan. To search for these, I continued running the Reservoir almost every day and I occasionally visited the northeast shore of Randall's Island.

Other than that, I was doing very little birding in late November and early December. The park did not hold anything I needed, and no one was reporting any birds new to me, not even Farnsworth, who did, however, find one bird that was new for *him*: a Northern Saw-whet Owl on November 23 in a small park in Sutton Place.

I also remember speaking to Starr during this period. She wanted to see the Northern Saw-whet Owl in Shakespeare Garden and the Barred Owl near the Great Lawn. She agreed to call me when she arrived in the afternoon and I would show her the roosts. When she did not call around the time I was expecting her, I called her. She had walked to the subway station and then realized that she would not have enough strength for the remaining ride and walk, so she had returned home. She was frustrated and sad. With more chemo scheduled the next day, she would not be able to see the owls anytime soon. It appeared that her condition was worsening, and I do not believe that she was able to visit Central Park again.

Finally, on December 3, Ben Cacace reported a bird that I needed, a White-winged Scoter seen flying off the northeast shore of Randall's Island. I went there and tried being more patient and watching this area for the scoter or other ducks, but I was unable to find anything.

I also made an early-December visit to Inwood Hill Park, which proved extremely disappointing. I thought that Spuyten Duyvil Creek might hold some interesting waterfowl, given that it was located just off the Hudson River and that it fed into a sheltered saltmarsh bay. But I saw very few birds and only a dozen species altogether.

Farnsworth's Saw-whet Owl had given him a two-bird lead, 204 to my 202, and that is how things still stood as of December 11.

41

COMMON REDPOLL

I was beginning to fear that Common Redpoll might follow the pattern set by many of the other irruptive finches this fall: appear initially to much fanfare, linger for a couple days, and then disappear. Only Pine Siskins continued to make frequent appearances in Central Park. Red Crossbills, Evening Grosbeaks, and White-winged Crossbills proved elusive. Common Redpolls, however, were generally more abundant than these other finches, and eBird maps had them showing up often to the north of New York City, so there was hope.

I had already seen a single Common Redpoll in April 2011, during my rookie year of birding, at the Evodia feeders. This bird was seen by many over a three-day period. The species itself usually shows up every two to three years in Central Park during finch irruptions. A small, drab bird, it would not excite birders anywhere near as much as Evening Grosbeak did. Still, people wanted to see it.

My second chance finally arrived on December 12. One of the park's regular birders posted a report online at 9:45 a.m. of a Common Redpoll feeding on a sweetgum tree in Mugger's Woods, in the Ramble, with American Goldfinches and Black-capped Chickadees.

I knew I did not have to hurry—fruiting trees were scarce in the park—but I made it into the Ramble by 10:30 a.m. I was not sure which sweetgum tree held the Redpoll, so I listened carefully as well as looked. I ended up making several circuits of the surrounding area before finally seeing the right tree, which was so much taller than I had expected that I did not immediately recognize it as a sweetgum. I had not seen its fruits dangling thirty feet or more above the ground.

The tree had various goldfinches and chickadees flitting about it. It took five minutes of scanning for me to find the female Common Redpoll, whose pale breast, dark streaking on the flanks, and tiny, light bill identified it without question.

Several more Common Redpolls appeared in this tree in the following days, giving everyone who wanted a chance to view this visitor from the Arctic.

It was my 203rd species of the year, and I was now only one behind Farnsworth. Game on, once again!

42

COMMON GOLDENEYE

With the last of the expected finches now on my list, my focus turned almost entirely back to ducks. I continued to run the Reservoir in search of Green-winged Teal and American Wigeon, and I checked the northeast shore of Randall's Island for White-winged Scoter and Surf Scoter.

The calendar was also opening up the opportunity for another species: Common Goldeneye. Some were seen at Pelham Bay Park, some miles north of Manhattan on the shore of the Atlantic, on December 11 and 12.

Common Goldeneye had only a small number of prior eBird reports in Manhattan, mostly in New York Harbor in the winter. The male is black and white with a round white spot on the face; the female has a gray body with a brown head. Most mature birds have yellow eyes, as you might guess from the name.

On my midday visit to Randall's Island on December 13, I got a close view of a male Common Goldeneye just off the northeast shore. This was the first sighting of the species in Manhattan during the fall season. It felt good again to be a finder and not just a chaser.

Of course it felt even better to have taken back a share of the big year lead! Farnsworth and I now were tied with 204 birds—

or so I thought.

I would not get to enjoy a share of the lead for long; in fact, I had really never had it. Farnsworth had observed a Common Redpoll of his own on November 27, but he did not enter it into eBird until December 15. I got to enjoy an illusory tie for two days, after which I was again one bird behind.

Farnsworth visited Randall's Island himself on December 16 and saw two female Common Goldeneyes. Now I was two birds behind again.

I had hoped that Farnsworth's extended absence from posting new species had signaled a long family vacation, perhaps somewhere far from Manhattan like the Galapagos Islands, where he could enjoy adding such exotic birds as Blue-footed Boobies to his world list[1] and give his Manhattan list—and me—a rest. No such luck.

At this point I would have been willing to buy him the tickets.

---

[1] It turns out Farnsworth already had Blue-footed Booby on his world list—and even on his United States list.

43

ICELAND GULL

Another duck species that sometimes appeared in December was the Canvasback. When it did, it was usually on the Hudson River, often near the shelter of a dock or pier. Jacob Drucker had observed it a number of times over the years in such locations. I wanted to see it, too, and soon! The year was drawing to a close.

I was just getting over a throat infection on December 17, and I wanted to take it easy. I planned on running at a modest pace across the city to 96th Street and the Hudson, and from there, following the river south to the 70th Street Pier. This would offer a chance to see not only a possible Canvasback but also gulls that perched on the docks and boats. Ben Cacace had observed an Iceland Gull at Randall's Island on the 15th, so the potential for unusual gulls, such as this one or even the Black-headed, was on my mind.

When I arrived at the Hudson around 1:50 p.m., I saw some sort of waterfowl well to the north, near 100th Street, so I ran toward it. It turned out to be just a Red-breasted Merganser.

The trip south had little to offer: Mallards, a Red-throated Loon, a Gadwall, and a Double-crested Cormorant.

I was near 68th Street at 2:27 p.m. when I heard my cell phone beeping. It was a bird alert—Jacob Drucker had just found a first-year Iceland Gull on the Reservoir near the west side pump house! I had stored his email address on my cell for just such emergencies, and I immediately texted him to please stay on the bird as I would be there in 15 minutes.

To get there that soon I would have to do what I had hoped to avoid: run fast, for over two miles, uphill. Motivating myself was easy, as I knew the Iceland Gull had no prior eBird records in Central Park (though it certainly had rarely occurred there; Starr Saphir, in particular, had it on her Central Park list).

I was relieved to see Drucker standing on the Reservoir running path when I arrived, with his binoculars out and his scope on his back. He assured me that the Iceland Gull was still there and challenged me to find it, a task made difficult both by the hundreds of gulls stationed along the reservoir's central dike (Drucker, using a clicking device, had just counted all the gulls exactly: 360 Ring-billed Gulls, and 350 Herring Gulls) and by the continual fogging of my binoculars from the body heat produced by hard running. I scanned around the general area in which Drucker appeared to be looking and eventually found the Iceland Gull, but I was not happy with the view—too far out and too many gulls in the way. He offered to bring out his scope, and, after some gull rearrangement, I saw the Iceland well. It had a rounded head, nearly all-dark bill, and overall pale plumage.

I was surprised that no one else responded to his alert. It was a very rare species for Manhattan, but apparently gulls do not generate as much excitement as the more colorful and better-known passerines. Iceland Gulls, as their name implies, visit the East Coast from their regular habitat in the North Atlantic.

I had again pulled to within one bird of Farnsworth, 205 to 206. I had three reasons to think that Farnsworth would not get the Iceland Gull: 1) he did not usually chase observations from Central Park, and he had not responded immediately to this one; 2) there were very few of these compared to thousands of other similar gulls, such as Ring-billed Gulls, and this one might not stick around; and 3) only two weeks remained to get it.

I shared my thoughts with Starr Saphir, who surprised me by saying that she had observed an Iceland Gull herself in November near the East River while returning from a medical appointment. She warned me that these gulls may not be as scarce as I had hoped.

44

AMERICAN WIGEON

As the days passed without Farnsworth entering an Iceland Gull, I grew more confident that he was not going to get it. The holidays were approaching, and perhaps my imagined scenario of him taking an end-of-year vacation somewhere outside New York County was not so farfetched.

Ducks were my last hope. On December 18 I rode the Staten Island Ferry in New York Harbor, looking for American Wigeon, Green-winged Teal, or Canvasback—the first two had been reported at Liberty State Park, which borders the harbor, earlier in the week. A long-shot possibility was Razorbill, which had been showing up recently at Coney Island. I did see a single, low-flying black-and-white bird, but I suspected it was a Bufflehead.

On the morning of December 20 I ran to check every large body of water in the north half of Central Park—the Meer, the Pool, the Reservoir, and Turtle Pond—for unusual ducks but did not see any.

As I was finishing my run, I received a personal text message from Jacob Drucker, who was asking if I had visited the likely *Selasphorus* hummingbird reported earlier that morning in Carl Schurz Park, not far from where I lived. I had not. Based on statistics, it was almost certainly a Rufous Hummingbird, and I did not have any camera, let alone one capable of photographing its fast-moving tail feathers in order to determine which species it was.

Drucker reminded me that this late in the season it could also be an Allen's Hummingbird, an Anna's Hummingbird, or a Calliope Hummingbird, so I told him I would take a look after lunch.

The location was near 87th Street and East End Avenue. After looking for 15 minutes, I finally noticed the hummingbird hovering high in the conifers ringing the Peter Pan statue. It never went lower to sample the very few nectar-filled flowers planted in the garden—odd behavior for a presumably hungry hummingbird. I saw it for about ten minutes, which was long enough to tell that it had a green back and rufous flanks. This meant it was not an Anna's, nor was it a Calliope. I entered it as a Rufous/Allen's Hummingbird in eBird, which would not add to my species total. But if someone later were to prove it was an Allen's, I would have a new species. It was certainly worth the effort.

On Friday, December 21, I did not do any morning birding. I was getting tired of running the Reservoir and seeing nothing, and I had to get ready to meet my girlfriend for a midday lunch.

As our lunch was ending I heard my cell phone beep. It was a text alert: Jacob Drucker had found an American Wigeon on the northwest cove of the Reservoir. As we walked back to my apartment, I explained that I would have to run out to the Reservoir quickly to get this bird. My girlfriend, who was not a birder, understood the importance of my big year, having heard my birding stories for many months now, and did not object to me changing into my running clothes and promising to be back in about a half-hour.

I ran along the bridle path, south of the Reservoir, and I soon saw Drucker and his scope across the grass. I yelled out, and he told me that the wigeon was right there, so I ran directly toward him and jumped the fence. There it was, close by the shore—white forehead, blue bill—a drake American Wigeon. It was a life Manhattan bird for him; I had seen one in October 2011 on Turtle Pond.

He also had the Iceland Gull in his scope, so I took another look at that. I thanked him for the excellent find, and explained that I had to return home right away.

Jacob Drucker's sharp, roving eyes had discovered two Reservoir rarities that were immensely valuable to me in my big year quest. You can see why I would much prefer to have him on my side than to have to compete against him.

I was in great spirits. I had regained a share of the big year lead with Farnsworth at 206 birds, and I had done it with American Wigeon, a bird that he had already listed. This was to my advantage because it meant that Farnsworth could not regain the outright lead simply by going to the Reservoir and seeing the wigeon. He would have to get some other bird, one that he did not already have.

45

FARNSWORTH'S FINAL SURGE

When I next checked the leader board on December 23, I was surprised to see Farnsworth ahead of me by one bird, at 207. How had he done that? I had not gotten any "Year Needs" alerts in the mean time, so he could not have observed a bird that was new to me—unless he had put it on a "hidden" list.

It appears that he birded Central Park on the late afternoon of the 22nd and saw the Barred Owl that had been roosting near the Pinetum. Of course—why wouldn't he? Any amateur could walk by, see a small crowd peering up—sometimes around someone with a scope pointing at the owl—and see it easily. It had been there well over a month. With the big year race this close, I could not expect Farnsworth to pass up a free bird.

I was not concerned about being one bird back. I still had just over a week to add one or two birds. A blast of cold weather was on the way, and this would likely encourage some of the ducks that were hanging out on upstate waters to move further south. Green-winged Teal were already being reported in large numbers in the New Jersey Meadowlands, just a few miles west of Central Park. A Snow Goose had been seen over Pelham Bay Park on the 23rd. Pine Grosbeak had been reported as far south as central Connecticut—chances were very slim, but it was a possibility here.

Snow was on the way, too, and this would encourage ground-feeding birds to move.

I continued running the Reservoir and seeing nothing new. The American Wigeon stayed only for a day.

Then I received some bad news and some worse news. The bad news: on Thursday, December 27, Farnsworth observed two Iceland Gulls in his regular early morning watch of the East River from Peter Detmold Park. This widened his lead to two birds.

The worse news: Farnsworth's lead somehow widened to *three* birds as of the 27th, and I could not tell what other species he added. It could not have been a species I lacked (again, unless it was "hidden"), and it was not something from his list containing the Iceland Gull. I searched the eBird database as many ways as I could, but I had no answer.

I had scrupulously entered each new species within a day of observing it, but I knew that Farnsworth sometimes entered a huge backlog of lists.

I also knew that this was the time of year to look back on your species list and check it for obvious gaps. Maybe you find that you are missing a fairly common bird like Indigo Bunting, one that you know you saw. Maybe you forgot to enter a day-list, or neglected to manually enter a rarity (common birds can simply be checked off a list).

Ultimately the explanation did not matter. Farnsworth now had 209 birds for the year. I had 206. It was December 28—time to see if I could stage a scoring drive of my own.

46

MY LAST-DAY RALLY

I spent Saturday, December 29, seeing my girlfriend. I felt that the big year pressure was finally off. I would need to observe three new birds in the two remaining days just to tie, and no one was reporting anything new. I doubted that many people were even birding, so I would almost certainly not have alerts to chase. I guessed that the odds of my pulling it off were roughly one in fifty.

If I was going to go out birding, it had to be somewhere that gave me a reasonable chance to add a specific new bird—it could not just be a random walk in the park.

Aside from the Reservoir, I believed that one of the best spots was the Hudson River. On December 27 three Canvasbacks had been observed on the New Jersey side of the Hudson at latitude 118th Street. Many more had been observed for weeks further north in Piermont. Perhaps the cold had finally driven some of them south.

Sunday, December 30, was near freezing with 40 mph wind gusts. Before noon I set out, walking along the Reservoir and then across the Upper West Side to 100th Street and the Hudson River. I followed the Greenway a little over two miles south to 59th Street. Conditions were terrible—ice patches on the path and cold winds blowing across the open water. The best birds I saw were two Common Loons.

Jacob Drucker meanwhile birded Central Park and came up with a respectable 42 species, including White-winged Crossbills and a flyover American Pipit. It surely would have been more pleasant to have spent the day in the more sheltered park, but none of those 42 birds would have done my big year list any good.

Just as I was finishing a gym workout, a 3:35 p.m. text alert arrived: someone was seeing a Common Raven at the café at Fort Tryon Park in Washington Heights. I was tempted to chase it, but I realized I had little chance of seeing the bird. I would need to change clothes at home, so at best I would leave at 3:50 and it would take me another 45 minutes, minimum, to reach the café. I would have only ten minutes of sunlight left, and, besides, Common Ravens were not known to perch for an hour. Almost certainly the bird would fly well before my arrival.

Farnsworth had taken a very early morning trip to Randall's Island and had seen some great birds, including a flock of American Pipits, an Iceland Gull, a Lesser Black-backed Gull, and several Common Goldeneyes, but none of these were new either to him or to me.

Later in the evening, just before 7 p.m., I received an eBird "Year Needs" email. Suddenly, my big year hopes were alive again.

Ben Cacace, one of the city's most accomplished birders, had gone to Randall's Island later in the afternoon and birded nearly all of it. He had observed a flock of 75 Horned Lark on the northwest baseball fields just after sunset. He had also seen three sparrow-like birds with white on the arm section of their wings, also after sunset, and could not positively identify them but suspected that they might be Snow Buntings.

Snow Buntings frequently mix in with flocks of Horned Lark,

so Cacace's suspicion made perfect sense.

I needed Horned Lark, which Farnsworth had already observed on his big day back in early November. Both of us needed Snow Bunting, which was extremely rare for Manhattan, with only one prior eBird record, a flyover in 2010 recorded by Farnsworth.

It is likely that snowfall north of Manhattan set these two birds and the pipits on the move.

I already knew my plan. Tomorrow, December 31, would be my last chance to wrest back the big year lead. I would go to Randall's Island early and try to get these two birds. Then, if I succeeded, I would go to the Chelsea waterfront in southwest Manhattan for one last try to get the Canvasback. Getting all three birds would tie me with Farnsworth—unless he managed to also get the Snow Bunting or, less likely, something else.

The large size of the Horned Lark flock was encouraging. Randall's Island provided an excellent habitat for the species: large, open fields with both short grass and bare ground. At least some remnants of the flock ought to remain on the 31st, I reasoned.

As for the Snow Buntings, I did not want to get my hopes too high. Cacace was not even sure he saw them, and what he did see he viewed in dim light.

December 31 turned out to be a pleasant day for birding, with a temperature just over freezing and calm to light winds. I put on my running gear with a polar fleece for extra warmth and by 10:15 a.m. I was out the door heading for the subway. I rode it to the Harlem-125th Street station, where I caught the waiting bus for a quick trip across the RFK Bridge.

I went to the northeast shore, scanning the fields for pipits on the way. As I looked out at the bay formed by the Bronx Kill, I saw the usual flock of hundreds of Brant. I also saw two Red-breasted Mergansers. I did not see any Common Goldeneye.

Cacace's Horned Larks had been on the northwest ball fields, so I started walking west. As I approached the bridge to the Bronx, I started hearing American Pipits and then saw 25 of them feeding on the adjacent field, tails bobbing.

Though I had observed these birds in flight before with Farnsworth at Inwood Hill Park, this was my first clear look at them on the ground at close range. They were skittish about my getting too close, however, so I stayed still or walked slowly.

On the northwest baseball fields I encountered some birds that were uncommon for this time of year, a lone Killdeer (which Cacace had reported) and a Belted Kingfisher, which I myself had often observed.

Further along I began to hear more high-pitched chatter, but it was different from that of the pipits. I looked around, and just fifty feet away were several Horned Larks, part of a flock of roughly 18. It was my first new species of the day!

I wanted to take my time to enjoy the close looks. I knew that I would not be seeing these birds often. They did not appear to be as concerned about my presence as the pipits were. The flock occasionally would fly a short distance to forage elsewhere, and I would tag along.

Soon I had my fill of this game, and the possibility of Snow Buntings came back to mind. More searching of the northwest ball fields did not reveal any, so I decided to give these fields a rest and walk back to the northeast shore, where I could look for more ducks.

I passed by the American Pipit flock again on the way back. It was thrilling to see these two species, pipits and larks, so abundant, as they almost never appeared in Central Park.

There were no new ducks on the bay, so I continued walking east along the shore. I heard Horned Larks again and saw another flock of 20 birds near the shoreline. I maneuvered around so that I was south of the flock and could view it in best light. Then I started to count the birds, one-by-one, focusing carefully on each bird. This decision yielded an unexpected reward. As I got toward the end of the line of birds, I noticed that one of them was not a Horned Lark at all—it was a Snow Bunting!

I examined it carefully, as I did not want to be wrong about such a mega-rarity, but there was no mistaking it—small yellow bill, cinnamon breast band (partial) and cheeks, white throat and belly. I had added species 208, bringing me to within one bird of Farnsworth.

I knew that my first responsibility was to report my sighting. It was OK to have waited on reporting the Horned Larks, as Ben Cacace's online posting the prior evening had announced the presence of a large flock, which people would reasonably assume to continue the next day. The Snow Bunting, however, was new, not mentioned in his post (only on his eBird report) and mine would be the first-ever eBird observation of the species on land in Manhattan.

At 12:05 p.m. I sent out a text alert on both of these birds. Then I quickly caught a bus back to Harlem and from there took the subway back to 86th Street.

My day was far from over. I needed to eat a quick lunch, post my observations online so that those who did not subscribe to the text alerts could also learn about the Snow Bunting, and then head for Chelsea.

I was not surprised to see Farnsworth soon send a text alert from Randall's Island noting the pipits and the Horned Lark. He had gone there from a nearby location immediately after my alert and had arrived just as I was leaving. What did surprise me was that he could not re-find the Snow Bunting. I had mixed feelings about this. I was glad to have a chance to tie for the big year lead with one more bird, but I was also hoping to have Farnsworth support my Snow Bunting observation with one of his own. He would do so the following morning.

I was back on the subway by 2:10 p.m., this time going downtown. At 53rd Street I transferred to the E line, which would take me to 14th Street and 8th Avenue, from which I would have just a short walk to the Hudson Greenway.

On the way I thought about the year that was coming to a close. I had run or walked over a thousand miles in 2012 in search of birds. My competition with Farnsworth and the others had begun with a frantic subway chase to observe rarities, and it was going to end that way, too.

The E train, which was headed toward Penn Station in Times Square, was packed with revelers. Their exit made the rest of the trip more relaxed, and soon I was emerging from underground on 14th Street.

It was 2:55 p.m. and the sun was still breaking through scattered clouds and shining on the Hudson. Pier 54 had wooden pilings supporting it along with many wooden beams projecting just above the water's surface. Ducks often like to hide on or around these pilings, so I scanned them carefully. I saw some Mallards and many Ring-billed Gulls and then continued moving south.

I also looked out further, toward the center of the Hudson a half-mile away. Canvasbacks might also appear there, and with my 10-power binoculars I would be able to identify them if they were well-lit.

I walked all the way out on the 10th Avenue Pier, roughly 300 yards, hoping that I would get a better view of the river's middle, but nothing interesting appeared. So I continued on south.

I was not seeing much—Gadwalls, Mallards, a small number of Great Black-backed Gulls, and a Double-crested Cormorant drying off on a piling. Further along I sighted a Common Loon just offshore.

The sun was moving closer to the horizon now, and I was aware of the implications, both practical and metaphorical! As I approached the small bay formed by Pier 25 and Nelson A. Rockefeller Park, I knew this was my last chance. Another Common Loon playfully dived for fish. Mallards congregated close to the shore. I saw nothing else.

No one in Manhattan had reported any Canvasbacks on the Hudson during the entire month of December. I could look farther, but what good would it do? I also could wait for a Common Raven to fly overhead or for a Razorbill to wander into New York Harbor, but this would be hoping for a miracle. I had an hour of sunlight left, but I saw no reason to use it. I wanted to beat the evening rush and go home.

My big year was over.

47

EPILOGUE

At the beginning of the year I thought I would do well to tally 175 birds and finish fourth among all Manhattan eBird users. By the end of an excellent spring season, I expected to reach 186. After a great fall season I finished at 208, having held first place from the end of January until the end of October. I never fell out of contention and finished twenty birds ahead of third place. I lost only to a vastly more knowledgeable and more skilled birder. I had done *much* better than I had expected.

My "lifetime" total of 214 for Manhattan, achieved in only two full years of birding, was the third highest on eBird, behind Andrew Farnsworth and Jacob Drucker.

The New York State Ornithological Association (NYSOA), a broad sample of birders, allows members to post their lifetime totals for the counties of New York State. As of 2011, my 214 would have ranked me fourth on this list, behind Peter Post (268), Lenore Swenson (244), and Jacob Drucker (222); in fact, only five[1] birders had submitted lifetime totals higher than my single-year total of 208.

Much of what made 2012 an unusually good year in which to see many species was beyond my control: a great spring warbler migration; a hurricane passing to the south; a series of strong finch and owl irruptions; and a widely-adopted text-alert system for rare birds. Of course the conditions were the same for everyone.

The only bird observed by more than a few people that I missed was Willow Flycatcher. There were other birds that I thought I should have had, such as Snow Goose, Green-winged Teal, White-winged Scoter, Common Raven, Golden Eagle, Greater Yellowlegs, Bank Swallow, and Vesper Sparrow, but these proved elusive for nearly everyone else, too.

I had not set any birding records, nor had I advanced the cause of science or commerce. I had, however, developed new skills to meet a very specific challenge. I had devised a well thought-out plan and put full effort into achieving it. I had spent my days healthfully, on my feet, in the beautiful parks of Manhattan. And, most of all, I had made up for many years of not looking.

---

[1] Some renowned Manhattan birders did not elect to report their lifetime totals on the NYSOA list, for example, Starr Saphir, whose lifetime Central Park total of 259 was, of course, entirely from Manhattan; or Irving Cantor, who had birded Manhattan since 1932 and who Starr believed might have the highest lifetime Manhattan total of any living birder; or Tom Fiore, a veteran birder who still posts some of the most extensive day lists and insightful commentary online. No doubt there are many others with high unreported totals.

Things I will remember:

- the hours of searching without finding, wondering if I would ever see another new bird; then the thrill of immediate recognition when one finally appeared.

- the adrenaline rush of a rare bird alert, of running fast and purposefully through the streets and the park.

- the spirited competition with Andrew Farnsworth and other top birders, which spurred me to doing my best.

- the birds, too, of course. I saw things few Manhattan-ites ever get to see: Common Nighthawks swooping across the sky for moths at dusk; Black Vultures and Bald Eagles soaring; Great Horned Owls roosting; Northern Gannets plunge-diving into the Hudson; and a Snow Bunting foraging on the ground with a flock of Horned Lark.

- their songs: the high *sweet, sweet, sweet, sweet, sweet* of the Prothonotary Warbler; the fluted *ee-oh-lay* and trill of a Wood Thrush; the explosive *Chick-chureer-eer-Chick* of a White-eyed Vireo.

- Starr Saphir's courageous struggle to continue leading her walks despite her illness. After an eleven-year battle, Starr succumbed to breast cancer in February 2013.

2012 was different from any other year in my life, and the novelty alone made it worthwhile. I can recall many years that were almost indistinguishable from others. This one stood out. It was a lot of fun and also very exhausting.

I will not be doing a big year again, at least not for a long, long time. It requires organizing one's life according to the whims of nature and the timing of other people's alerts. At the start of 2013 I was looking forward to taking control of my schedule again, to returning to my work, and to writing this book.

I wanted to bird more casually and at the same time expand my Manhattan life list. The Reservoir in late January 2013 provided several opportunities for the latter: a lingering Common Merganser (possibly the same one later found on the Meer); a Black-headed Gull; and a bird that I circled the Reservoir so many times in November and December trying to find, a Green-winged Teal.

Great timing, Green-winged Teal—where were you when I needed you?

There were other rarities that I had missed in 2012 but that occasionally appeared in Manhattan, and I was already thinking about how I would find them.

APPENDIX

EXAMINING WARBLER FREQUENCY

2012 was an unusually good year for observing warblers in Manhattan. Birders had multiple chances to respond to reports of even the rarest such species.

There are, in total, 36 warbler species that regularly pass through Central Park in either the spring or the fall. Of these, two, denoted by an (f) below, occur most often in the fall: Connecticut Warbler and Golden-winged Warbler.

1   Ovenbird
2   Worm-eating Warbler
3   Louisiana Waterthrush
4   Northern Waterthrush
5   Golden-winged Warbler (f)
6   Blue-winged Warbler
7   Black-and-white Warbler
8   Prothonotary Warbler
9   Tennessee Warbler
10 Orange-crowned Warbler
11 Nashville Warbler
12 Connecticut Warbler (f)

13 Mourning Warbler
14 Kentucky Warbler
15 Common Yellowthroat
16 Hooded Warbler
17 American Redstart
18 Cape May Warbler
19 Cerulean Warbler
20 Northern Parula
21 Magnolia Warbler
22 Bay-breasted Warbler
23 Blackburnian Warbler
24 Yellow Warbler
25 Chestnut-sided Warbler
26 Blackpoll Warbler
27 Black-throated Blue Warbler
28 Palm Warbler
29 Pine Warbler
30 Yellow-rumped Warbler
31 Yellow-throated Warbler
32 Prairie Warbler
33 Black-throated Green Warbler
34 Canada Warbler
35 Wilson's Warbler
36 Yellow-breasted Chat

Of course, some are much easier to observe than others. The analytics on eBird allow you to assign a number to rarity. I like to look at "peak frequency." In other words, pick the best week of the year for observing the species in a given area and then ask what percentage of birding lists submitted in that week have the species on them. I used data from 2008 to 2011.

One of the commonest warblers is the Yellow-rumped Warbler. Its peak frequency occurs historically during the first week of May, when 69% of birder-submitted lists have at least one Yellow-rumped Warbler on them. The American Redstart is another easy bird, with a peak frequency of 68% during the second week of September.

The Chestnut-sided is somewhere in the middle between common and rare: it peaks at 30% in the spring and 23% in the fall. The Nashville peaks at 31% in the first week of May and 9% during the fall.

Among the rarer warblers are the Blackburnian and the Prairie—both peak at around 23% in the first week of May and do not get above 6% in the fall. The Cape May peaks at 17% during the second week of May, and the Bay-breasted peaks at 13% in the third week of May, and neither gets above 3.4% in the fall. All of these warblers are good candidates for text alerts when observed.

Then there are the very rare warblers. The Hooded peaks at 7% in late April and early May and less than 3% in the fall (at least until 2012!). The Mourning peaks at 7% in the spring and is rarely observed in the fall.

Not so, however, in 2012, when Mournings appeared frequently in the spring in both Central and Bryant Parks, and then one continued in the Ramble in August and September.

The Worm-eating is only a bit less rare, peaking at 10% in the first week of May. This year a very cooperative Worm-eating Warbler hung out in the Upper Lobe from early June through early September, making the species look much more common than it usually is.

The six rarest warblers are rarer still; they are "scarce," and are not recorded every year in Central Park.

Here they are, along with their peak frequencies:

1	Kentucky Warbler	2.2
2	Connecticut Warbler	2.4
3	Golden-winged Warbler	2.9
4	Yellow-thoated Warbler	3.5
5	Prothonotary Warbler	4.5
6	Cerulean Warbler	4.5

I would not put much significance on the relative differences between them in peak frequencies as the number of observations of each is too low. Let's just agree that all of these are very, very rare. You could bird regularly for a decade in the park and still not have all of them on your life list, and I know of birders for whom this is the case.

What makes 2012 so unusual is that many of these rarest warblers were reported frequently and seen often.

Prothonotary Warbler was reported at least five times in Central Park, and there was a Prothonotary that lingered at Bryant Park for over a week.

Cerulean Warbler was reported four times in Central Park (one was found by Starr by the Meer) and once in Riverside Park.

Yellow-throated Warbler had a widely-seen appearance in Riverside Park and at least two others in Central Park.

A Kentucky Warbler lingered around the Shakespeare Garden area for over a week beginning in late April; another appeared in May in the North End. In late August yet another lingered by the Loch. This is amazing, considering how many years that the Kentucky Warbler does not appear in Central Park at all.

You can read in Chapter 31 about occurrences of Connecticut and Golden-winged.

Now, on to the central question of this appendix: why were rare warblers observed and reported so much more frequently in Manhattan in 2012 than in recent years?

It is certainly not because there suddenly were more of them, at least not in terms of total species population. Since the mid-1960s many warbler species have experienced drastic declines; the Cerulean Warbler population has fallen by 80%. Starr Saphir tells of having seen single trees with forty Prairie Warblers in them in the 1970s. Now one rarely sees even three together. Habitat loss is the main culprit.

As mentioned in Chapter 22, many migrants have responded to global warming by breeding further north. For those that already were breeding well north of Manhattan, this should not affect how many of them pass through. But some species—Prothonotary and Kentucky Warblers, for example—generally nest to the south of New York and occur here only when they "overshoot" their target and end up too far north. Perhaps more of them are now encouraged to choose a more northern breeding location, which would increase the likelihood of overshoots reaching New York. In birds observed so rarely, even a small increase in the number arriving leads to a noticeable difference in apparent abundance. Whether or not something like this is happening is a question I am not able to answer.

I can speak to another change that I believe explains some of the observed increase: better and more widely-used technology. Today nearly every birder carries a cell phone and many have smart phones. Birders can immediately transmit noteworthy observations to others via the text alert system or the online message boards. This is something that was not being done five years ago, even if many people already had smart phones—the level of adoption among birders, a group that tends to be older and less eager to embrace new technology, was low.

Now birders feel comfortable sending and receiving text messages, and they also know how to monitor relevant internet sites, both in the field and at home, for up-to-the-minute reports on what other birders are observing. Each birder becomes a perceptual element in a large network of birders. When you go into Central Park you rely not only on your own eyes and ears but also on dozens of other pairs to help you find the few birds out of thousands that are of greatest interest.

As a result "peak frequency" no longer carries as much meaning about species abundance: when one birder observes a rare bird, other birders are quickly called to the scene and they observe it, too.

The site eBird saw a 45% yearly increase in lists submitted in 2012, showing that more birders are interested in electronically reporting and listing what they observe. With this comes a feedback loop: birders who use eBird's alert features learn immediately the precise details of relevant observations, making it more likely that they can find these birds in a timely manner and also report them.

Index

H

I

J

K

L

M

T

ABOUT THE AUTHOR

David Barrett earned his undergraduate degree in mathematics from Harvard, and did graduate work in mathematics at MIT and in finance at the University of Chicago. His career has been as a trader and hedge fund manager. Other interests include competitive running, bodybuilding, solving crossword puzzles, and, of course, birding. His lifetime total of 241 bird species in Manhattan, where he lives, places him second on eBird's all-time list as of December 2014.

Visit the site for him and this book at www.bigmanhattanyear.com.

CPSIA information can be obtained at www.ICGtesting.com
Printed in the USA
LVOW04s0518150415

434630LV00019BB/336/P